YOUR
TICKET TO
NEW TRADITIONS
★ ★ ★ ★ ★

Family
FUN
NIGHT

CIDER MILL
PRESS

BOOK
PUBLISHERS

Kennebunkport, Maine

13-Digit ISBN: 9781604336115

10-Digit ISBN: 1604336110

This book may be ordered by mail from the publisher. Please include $5.95 for postage and handling. Please support your local bookseller first!

Books published by Cider Mill Press Book Publishers are available at special discounts for bulk purchases in the United States by corporations, institutions, and other organizations. For more information, please contact the publisher.

Cider Mill Press Book Publishers

"Where good books are ready for press"

PO Box 454
12 Spring Street
Kennebunkport, Maine 04046

Visit us on the Web! www.cidermillpress.com

Cover design by Shelby Newsted and Abbie Masso
Interior design by Jon Chaiet
Typeset in Verlag

Printed in the United States

1 2 3 4 5 6 7 8 9 0

First Edition

For my dad, who always puts family first

START

ACKNOWLEDGMENTS

This book could not have been completed without the dedication of my outstanding editor, Alexandra Lewis. Her suggestions, research assistance, and creative guidance were crucial throughout the writing process.

Many thanks to my clever and creative designer, Jon Chaiet, as well as Charlotte Gross and Emma Lamberton, who helped revise the book and who also generated terrific ideas for new ways to have family fun!

TABLE OF CONTENTS

SECTION 2: THE ACTIVITIES

INTRODUCTION

You may think it's the weeklong trip to Disneyland that your kids will remember, but it's more likely that they will recall the demented chicken that Dad drew during an all-play turn in Pictionary® or the fact that Mom had the worst poker face when playing Blind Man's Bluff. We remember the silly bonding moments, the times we felt a real connection as a family, the laughter. It doesn't matter whether your family likes to play Monopoly® or musical instruments, make pizza or photo placemats. What matters is that your family establishes a regular time to have fun, enjoy one another's company, and create lasting memories. I'm hopeful that the ideas in this book will encourage your family to start your own unique Family Fun Night traditions.

In this new edition, we've updated all of the content that made the first book a hit with families, and we've added some entirely new material. We've also created a website (www.FamilyFunNight.org) that allows us to provide readers with information that is current, including links to useful sites. You'll also find book, movie, and video game lists, which will be updated frequently. The website also allows you to share your own ideas and memories with us!

This book is divided into two sections. The first offers general information about game nights: ways to engage the kids, age-appropriate activities, and rules to make things run more smoothly. The second details specific game nights your family might enjoy. You can follow one plan from start to finish, or you can choose bits and pieces from each game night, mixing and matching to suit your family's needs. Sidebars include tips to enhance the fun, personal stories to inspire families, and a little history lesson now and then.

I hope you'll enjoy making wonderful family memories together, one night at a time!

Cindy

WHY FAMILY FUN NIGHT?

Generations of parents and kids have insisted that they value time together more than anything else, but busy schedules and a host of other commitments have often gotten in the way. The number of families eating dinner together on a regular basis has dropped steadily over the past 30 years and recently, even "togetherness" rarely means meaningful conversation, with cell phones and tablets distracting even the youngest members of the family.

But things may be changing. Due in part to lessons learned from the recession of 2008, family values and family activities are beginning to coincide. Staying in has become the new going out, with "cocooning" more appealing to many families as budgets tighten and money allocated for entertainment shrinks. In greater numbers, multiple generations are living together under one roof, meaning that there are more people in a household who can interact with one another. As a result of these shifts, board game sales have soared recently. Families are rediscovering the simpler pleasures of each other's company.

TIDBIT

Back in 2005, a Gallup poll asked people to name their favorite way to spend an evening. The most popular response? Staying home with the family (32%), which beat out watching television and reading, numbers two and three.

TIDBIT

The folks in Ridgewood, NJ inspired other communities nationwide when they declared March 26, 2002 to be "Family Night." Teachers were asked not to assign homework, coaches were expected to cancel practices and games, school performances were moved to different days—even town and school meetings were postponed. Watching television was forbidden. A follow-up survey found that most Ridgewood families appreciated the evening that was devoted to family bonding.

It's true that many things continue to compete for our attention, even at home: TV, video games, texting friends, and checking Facebook. Teenagers, especially, will always be drawn to their peers; it's a natural and necessary part of growing up. But family members are starting to have a greater appreciation for one another, establishing new traditions centered around old-fashioned family values.

MY STORY

"I find that we learn a lot more about our kids' lives during game night than at any other time. Their defenses are down and they tend to chat about things that they would normally not share with us. Conversation is easier than when we're quizzing them about their day-to-day activities."

—*Lakisha, mother of three*

CHAPTER TWO

GETTING EVERYONE ON BOARD

Most children are excited about the idea of family night. For a six-year-old, an evening spent playing cards with Mom and Dad is about as good as it gets! Once you establish the tradition, they will be counting down to the next Family Fun Night.

If they seem less than enthusiastic, take them to the store or go online and let them select a new board game. Or begin with a movie night (see Chapter 11) and allow your most reluctant child to choose the film.

It will take a while for everyone to get used to the idea of regularly setting aside time away from TV, cell phones, and video games. Your attitude is contagious, though, and as long as you act excited (and not stressed out) about the idea, your kids will follow your lead.

MY STORY

"Initially, we had trouble getting everyone together. We were too hung up on the idea of a Friday or Saturday night. When we discovered that late afternoon on Sunday seemed to be a more convenient time for everyone, we were able to start a real tradition."

—*Nancy, mother of two*

You're not trying to recreate a three-ring circus or amusement park experience; you're just going for some fun and relaxation with the people who mean the most to you.

MY STORY

"The trick is to focus on the fun of family night, not make it one more thing on the to-do list."

—*Barry, father of three*

• • •

"My seven-year-old idolizes a girl in her class named Sarah whose mother I know well. I asked my friend if we could borrow one of Sarah's favorite board games for our first family night and my daughter couldn't wait to learn how to play!"

—*Dana, mother of one*

SEVEN WAYS TO GET KIDS EXCITED ABOUT FAMILY FUN NIGHT

1. Use sticky notes to remind everyone about the fun evening you have planned: Come up with clever phrases that will entice them and affix the notes to bathroom mirrors, computer screens, and dinner plates leading up to the designated evening.

2. Save mementos from activities you've done together in the past (like a funny sketch from Pictionary) and hang them in prominent places with a note: "Who remembers this 'dog' that looks just like a horse?"

3. If your kids enjoy competition, set up Family Fun Night as a series of rounds in a tournament that will lead to a championship round.

(continued on next page)

(continued from previous page)

4. Reward winners with tickets that can be exchanged for small prizes. Establish a rule that before the "prize center" opens for business, every child must have tickets to redeem.

5. Alter games to suit your family's interests. If your daughter loves horses, buy her a small horse that is her own special token for Monopoly.

6. Get together with another family whose kids are favorites of your children.

7. Allow anxious children to start by watching as the rest of the family plays. It won't be long before they are begging to be included.

TIP

Prizes don't have to cost a thing! How about offering up an extra half hour of TV on a Sunday morning, an extra half hour added to bedtime, a bonus bedtime story, or the privilege of riding in the front seat of the car for a whole week?

If you have a stepfamily, it can be a challenge to line up everyone's schedules because often there isn't daily communication. One way to ensure that everyone will be together is to plan family nights for weekends when you take the whole crew out of town. Removing kids from their peer groups will allow them to connect with the family. If staying in a hotel is not an option, trade houses with an out-of-town family or stay with friends or relatives.

Pre-teens and teens can be harder to get on board than younger kids. Despite the fact that in a recent YMCA poll, 21 percent of teens listed "not having enough time together with parents" as their most significant concern, it's natural for them to resist spending a Friday or Saturday night at home. Ignore their grumbling! You can allow reluctant participants to invite a friend or start the tradition with a video game night (see the Tidbit on page 20) if they'll agree to play a classic board game the next time the family gets together. Or propose a "cool" game that they are likely to want to learn how to play, like poker. Use real poker chips so they'll feel like they're part of an adult game.

MY STORY

"We had the best family nights when we stayed in my parents' guest house. There was no TV, no Internet, nothing but a cabinet full of games, cards, and books. With limited cell service, even texts weren't blowing up our phones. We all felt relaxed and free to enjoy each other's company."

—*Cathy, mother of three, stepmother of three*

TIP

Teens will do just about anything—even homework—if they can listen to their favorite music while doing it. Perhaps for the first family get-together, you can allow them to choose the background music. One parent said that her teens liked rap (which she couldn't tolerate) so they compromised on Spanish rap, which had the beat her kids liked but no one was offended because they didn't understand the lyrics!

TIDBIT

Are your middle schoolers reluctant to give up their video games for a night of family fun? No problem! Start your Family Fun Night tradition with a video game night! In 2013, researchers at ASU found that when parents shared the gaming experience with their kids, they reported improved communication and bonding within the family. Researchers advised parents not to miss an opportunity to play family video games, suggesting that they consciously turn gaming into a point of conversation rather than conflict.

Lure teens with rewards they will appreciate: The night's grand prize can be an extra hour added to a Saturday night curfew, use of the car keys for a night, first rights to the bathroom every morning for a week, a video game party with friends, or a sleepover.

Once you have established a consistent family night, most teens won't require bribes. But don't feel guilty about doing what you need to at first so that they'll stay connected to family. They won't realize (until they're a little older) that the real reward of taking part in family night is the bond they strengthen with you and with their siblings, and the great memories they'll have.

MY STORY

"We had trouble getting our teenage sons interested in game night. Finally we bought a dartboard and darts and said that we were having a tournament. They loved the idea! It's just adult enough to appeal to them."

—*Mike, father of two*

read-aloud night
card sharks night
board game night
video game night
movie night
charity night

CHAPTER THREE

HOUSE RULES

You'll want to establish some general rules for family night to prevent arguments and avoid confusion. Basically, the rules are intended to make sure that everyone in the family attends cheerfully, that there are no distractions, and that everyone understands how each game is played.

To start, how will you determine what each week's activity will be? Maybe you'll want to take turns choosing. This works best if children select from a master list of games and activities (rather than from their vast imaginations). If you elect to do this, the person who makes the selection can be in charge of setting up the game or activity, explaining the rules, and cleaning up. Another option—one with an element of surprise—is to pull ideas written on slips of paper from a Family Fun Night jar. Creative folks can make their own game spinner with an arrow that will point to the chosen activity. Inevitably, some in the group will be happy with the choice and some won't be. But an important rule that you'll want to enforce from the start is that everyone will participate with a positive attitude and an open mind.

TIP

If everyone agrees, you can have special rules for the younger kids in the family. For a game of volleyball, for instance, you can allow kids under five to pick up the ball and throw it over the net.

Rules to Play By

For game night to run smoothly, the rules of each activity need to be articulated and understood by everyone. It doesn't matter whether you follow the rules as they are written for an individual game or you decide to make up your own, they just need to be agreed upon by all players.

If you choose to develop your own rules, you'll need to write them down. You may want to start a journal in which you write down the rules you've agreed upon for various games. That way, you can look them up in the event of a disagreement. Children must also understand the importance of everyone following the same rules. When the rules have been established, a parent can read them aloud, and then the family can play one round as a practice round to be sure everyone understands.

If it's necessary to choose teams, a parent may want to make the assignments so that the sides are evenly matched. This doesn't mean that the numbers need to be even: You can pit the family's chess champ against the rest of the group. Even if teams aren't required, they can be helpful when there is a significant age spread. A board game like Monopoly can be played as a team game. For games involving more luck than skill, names can be drawn from a hat. In games of chance, the kids may get a kick out of teaming up against the parents. If it seems like that would work out, let them go for it!

Although a team can work with members simply rotating turns and decision-making, in the case of a mixed age team, it's probably best to choose a team leader who, after consulting with the other members, will make the final decision on a move or a play.

Finally, you'll need to decide how to handle cheating. What should the consequences be? It's less emotional if the ground rules are established before the situation arises. You might have the person who cheated miss the next turn or lose a certain number of points. It's trickier if a player is accused of cheating and vehemently denies it. If there is no consensus that cheating occurred, you may simply have to continue the game, with a general reminder that a victory based on cheating is no victory at all.

TIP

HOW TO RESOLVE DISAGREEMENTS DURING A GAME:

- For every game, appoint a judge who will make a decision if there is a stalemate (allow two minutes for the disputing parties to work it out themselves before the judge gets involved)

- Flip a coin

- Re-play the round in question

CHAPTER FOUR

SPORTSMANSHIP

Family Fun Night offers lots of opportunities to teach important lessons about winning and losing gracefully, taking turns, following rules, and using good manners. Teaching and practicing these skills happens naturally within the context of playing games.

TIDBIT

Should parents let kids win? Most parents and child-rearing experts agree that parents shouldn't play a game poorly in order to let a child win. There is not much to be gained by doing that. The best idea is to change the rules so that the playing field is even: Start the child off with extra letters in Scrabble or extra points in badminton. If the age spread is very wide, create even teams. That way, both parents and kids can try their hardest and enjoy the game.

It can be difficult to convey the message to our kids that winning isn't everything. Parents are up against powerful media messages about the value of winning (magazine covers and tickertape parades are reserved for the winners, not the runners-up). As adults, we know the truth behind the familiar adage stressing "how you play the game," but that can be a tricky concept for little folks to embrace. It's important, though, to make it clear from the start that boastful winners and sore losers are not acceptable on game night.

A game winner can certainly celebrate, but parents might need to remind him to do so without making the other players feel inferior. After all, no one wins every game, and it's likely that the winner of this game won't be the winner of the next. Establish a tradition around winning that recognizes and rewards the victory, but also contains it. Others might congratulate the winner with a high five, or allow the winner to go first in the next round, or choose the next game.

Those who don't win need to accept the outcome gracefully. Remind them to study the strategies used by the winners in order to try them in the next round. It's been said many times that people learn more from failure than from success, so kids should regard a loss as an opportunity to improve their own skills. Remind everyone that the real winners are those who have a great time, learn something new, realize the satisfaction of trying their hardest, and enjoy the time spent with family. No one's going to remember who won round four of Scrabble on the third Friday in March.

You can help your child respond appropriately throughout the night by employing a strategy that is based on his or her temperament. An emotional child must learn to compose and calm himself before reacting to a situation; you can tell him to count silently to 10 before responding or to notice clues about himself when he is getting upset so that he can avoid inappropriate behavior. Children who are perfectionists need to be reminded about all of the things they've accomplished, learned and done correctly, not the ways in which they fell short. Kids who act out when things don't go their way need to be warned about the specific consequences of inappropriate behavior, such as sitting out during the next round due to a temper tantrum.

The most significant thing that parents can do is to model good behavior. Offer praise and encouragement to all players, and take winning and losing in stride. Show your kids that you can enjoy something (foosball, maybe?) without necessarily being great at it. Look for teachable moments throughout the course of the evening, and reinforce humility and empathy whenever possible.

CHAPTER FIVE

ACTIVITIES FOR ALL AGES

It's important to choose activities that are appropriate for the ages of your kids. Most games have a recommended age range, which will help you decide. In addition, there are some general age-group guidelines that will prove useful when you are determining what might be the most fun for your family.

Three and Under

For the littlest tykes, the best games are open-ended and can be adapted as play continues. You may find that you and your child establish your own rules rather than play by the rules that come with the game. Ideal games are ones where chance is a more significant factor than skill or physical ones with simple rules. Each game should be relatively short, allowing you to play several rounds or several different games in one night. Try games like Go Away Monster!®, Bob the Builder: Scoop's Construction Site Game®, Haba Orchard Game® (note choking hazard), and Cranium Cariboo®.

TIP

One way to include a young child in a Family Fun Night with older kids is to team her up with a parent or older sibling, or give her tasks such as rolling the dice, turning over a sand timer, or moving game pieces.

Four- and Five-Year-Olds

This is a good time to begin playing games that require taking turns, sharing, and following simple rules. Activities involving fantasy, imagination, and creativity are especially popular with four- and five-year-olds.

Look for board games that don't require players to read, like Chutes and Ladders® and Candyland®. Clue Little Detective Game®, in which players match colors rather than read words, is perfect for pre-readers and will prepare them for more advanced games of Clue®. Hungry, Hungry Hippos®, Don't Spill the Beans® and Don't Break the Ice® are also fun games intended for kids in this age group. If they want to play more adult games, simplify the rules and shorten the game so that they can be included.

Six- to Nine-Year-Olds

Children six to nine are able to pay attention for longer stretches of time and will start to show an interest in more adult board games. They understand concepts of teamwork and have a keen interest in rules and rituals, sometimes preferring to develop complicated sets of rules of their own. Because they can hold a hand of cards, add up points on dice, and cope with losing, family games become more enjoyable for everyone involved. Fantasy begins to play a smaller role with school-age kids and real-life situations become of greater interest. Craft projects are popular, and kids enjoy making jewelry they can wear or duct tape wallets they can take to school. They enjoy the sense of accomplishment that comes from seeing a project through from start to finish.

MY STORY

"We try to reinforce skills they are learning at school during our game nights. If they are excited about writing, we let them write the script for a puppet show. If science is something they are involved in at school, we'll try some simple science experiments. We find they're more enthusiastic about family night if we let their areas of interest guide us as far as the activities we choose."

—*Sandy, mother of three*

Simple card games and many board games appeal to kids in this age range. Several different versions of Clue Jr., based on the adult board game Clue, use symbols as well as words so that kids who are just learning to read can solve the puzzles. Heads Up® is a game (also available as an app) developed by Ellen DeGeneres that's a lot of fun for families with kids eight and older. Oodles of Doodles® is a simple, fast-paced introduction to more complicated drawing games, such as Pictionary. Active play is important to kids of this age also. Games like Twister® are great and can be played outdoors as well as indoors. They also like throwing at targets and enjoy games involving running, like TV tag, in which kids must sit down and call out the name of a television character in order to be safe from being tagged. You may also want to find ways to pull kids into non-competitive activities like jigsaw puzzles or family scavenger hunts.

Pre-Teens

Pre-teens develop strong preferences of their own about what kinds of games and activities they want to play. They can be very competitive in these years, and long for challenging strategic and skill-based games. They are able to win and lose with grace, so parents don't have to referee too often. Middle schoolers enjoy games like Are You Smarter Than a 5th Grader®? and trivia games intended for their age group. Monopoly is popular with older kids, as is Apples to Apples®, The Game of Life®, and Pictionary. Scattergories® and Taboo® are terrific team games for older kids, and Say Anything® is fun because there are no right or wrong answers.

MY STORY

"We let our teen-agers select the games we play for our game nights. They usually end up teaching us the rules of some card game they learned from friends, which is an interesting role-reversal. They like being in charge."

—Maria, mother of two

Teens and Twenty-Somethings

Hanging with teens and twenty-somethings can be even more fun for parents than spending an evening with friends: The options are truly endless! The older your kids are, the more they will enjoy reminiscing: Spend a few hours looking through family photos or watching old home movies. Active games like HORSE, Ping-Pong, and bowling also appeal to this age group, as do more cerebral board games like Dixit® and edgier ones like Cards Against Humanity® and the Would You Rather Board Game®. If your older kids like to invite friends or significant others to join in the family fun—and they don't embarrass easily—try Game for Fame® or Rollick®, the Hysterical Game of Clues and Collaboration.

CHAPTER SIX

TREATS FOR FAMILY FUN NIGHT

Family Fun Night just wouldn't be the same without a favorite meal or some special snacks. The evening will be especially meaningful to the kids if you invite them into the kitchen: They can assist with the planning, shopping, cooking, and serving. Even though it's a bit more work when kids "help" prepare food, they bring enthusiasm and a refreshing attitude into the kitchen. They are fascinated by how a list of mysterious ingredients like baking soda and shredded lemon peel can combine to create a delicious dish. For them, cooking is less like a chore and more like magic or a really neat science experiment!

FIVE THINGS TO HAVE ON HAND FOR LITTLE CHEFS

- A step stool

- A kid-size apron

- Hair ties for pulling hair up and out of the way

- Different colored measuring cups and spoons

- Small spoons, spatulas, and other kid-size utensils

To make the kids-in-the-kitchen idea work, you'll want to do two things: One is plan ahead, and the other is lower your standards. Prepare for your little helpers by having specific tasks in mind for them to do and by taking care of much of the work ahead of time. Try to avoid having kids standing around waiting while you tackle a complicated part of the recipe. Before small kids join you in the kitchen, you may want to chop, slice, or puree ingredients, measure them into small bowls, or wash fruits or vegetables.

Think about how your kids will be able to contribute and what tasks you can assign to them. Little ones love to stir, knead dough, wash produce, tear lettuce, roll meat into balls, and set the table. Five- to seven-year-olds will be able to take on even more responsibility: They can also read instructions from a recipe card aloud, measure and pour ingredients, and help find things in the kitchen.

Older children will be able to cut vegetables, cheese, or bread; crack eggs; and use a microwave oven or food processor. They will also enjoy putting bite-size pieces of food on skewers. Urge kids who are learning about fractions in school to use their newfound skills to measure ingredients. If they're studying the food pyramid in health class, they can assess the meal and see how it stacks up.

Most teenagers are capable of handling everything themselves, from choosing a recipe to cooking and serving an entire meal. They may want to create their own recipes, test out an exotic or ethnic dish, or alter existing recipes to make them vegan or gluten-free. Encourage their creativity!

MY STORY

"My son always wants to experiment by adding funky ingredients to whatever it is we're making. To avoid ruining an entire meal, I set out a small plastic bowl for him with a portion of the food in it and let him do whatever he wants. Then he can cook or bake his own creation, try it out, and decide if he likes his recipe alterations."

—Eva, mother of one

Once the meal is underway, relax. Let the kitchen get messy. Don't shoot for a Julia Child creation, just go for edible and interesting. You and the kids will have more fun if you can ignore the sticky floor and the puddle of milk next to the canister set. (Just make sure to include the kids in the clean up, too!)

You can lighten up about the mess, but be vigilant about safety: Always turn the handles of pots and pans inward so that little kids can't reach up and grab them, and position kids so that they can't reach any appliances or anything sharp. Rather than inundate your children with a list of dos and don'ts, most of which they won't remember, establish a few basic rules, such as:

wash your hands before you begin cooking

don't touch knives without permission

don't use the stove unless supervised

Suggestions for snacks and special dishes to complement many of the Family Fun Night ideas are included here. However, most kids are just as delighted with take-out food. Most family restaurants offer anything on the menu as a to-go item. If you'd rather focus on the activity than the food, order in (and treat yourself!).

Outdoor Picnic

It's hard to go wrong with a picnic basket full of food and drinks, a bucolic setting, and a host of delightful games for your family to play!

Your best bet is to head for a public park with pavilions, picnic tables, and built-in barbeque grills.

Whether you bring along a gourmet spread or peanut butter and jelly sandwiches, food eaten outdoors just tastes better! Keep it simple (think bite-size whenever possible), and bring just what you'll eat and no more. A deli bar is easy and popular: Pack assorted meats, cheese, rolls, condiments and pasta salads in vinegar-based marinades. Round out the meal with pretzels or chips, carrot and celery sticks, grapes, slices of watermelon, and cookies or Rice Krispie Treats®. Cold chicken is another picnic favorite, served with a side of potato salad and fresh fruit kabobs. Trail mix is a great pre- or post-meal snack.

You can certainly have a traditional cookout with burgers and hot dogs, but you'll have to pay special attention to keeping meat cold until it's time to put it on the grill. You'll also have to be prepared for a wait as the charcoal heats up.

TIP

For a picnic, don't forget to bring:

- garbage bags
- cap opener, bottle opener
- serving spoons
- serrated knife, cutting board
- folding chairs
- wipes to clean up after the meal
- roll of paper towels
- plastic wrap, baggies, and plastic containers for leftovers
- picnic blanket

TIPS FOR COOKING ON A CHARCOAL GRILL

- Marinate the meat the night before and wrap it in plastic wrap.

- Use a wire brush to clean the grill.

- With a paper towel, rub a little vegetable oil on the grill so the meat doesn't stick.

- Use an electric charcoal lighter rather than lighter fluid to avoid adversely affecting the food's flavor.

- When the coals are red, spread them out using tongs. For direct cooking, coals are spread evenly over the bottom of the grill; for indirect cooking, the charcoal is placed on the sides of the grill bottom, but not in the center. After about 20 minutes, the coals will turn white-ish; then they're ready. Cedar chips for flavoring can be placed directly on coals or in a perforated foil pouch under the grill surface.

- Cook hot dogs, hamburgers, corn on the cob, and potatoes over direct heat. Thicker meats like steak and chicken quarters can be cooked over indirect heat. Allow four minutes on each side for a burger, and cook chicken pieces much longer, until the juices run clear. Use a meat thermometer to test for doneness: It should read 170 degrees for breast meat and 180 degrees for thighs and drumsticks.

- Turn the meat after one side has finished cooking; when cooked through, remove the meat with a clean set of tongs.

THE BEST TIPS FOR PICNIC DINNERS

IN ADVANCE

- Freeze water bottles to pack between (not just under) food items; they will keep food cold but will melt by the end of the evening for cold drinking water

- Save individual packets of mayo, mustard, and ketchup from fast food restaurants to bring on the picnic

- Make sure the chosen location does not have restrictions that will affect your plan (regarding barbeque grills, pets, swimming...)

ON THE DAY OF

- Envision yourself at the picnic site eating the meal to make sure you don't forget to pack something critical, like a serving spoon or bottle opener

- Pack foods to be eaten last on the bottom of the cooler

- Bring two coolers, one for drinks and one for food (because the one holding drinks will be opened more often)

- Use pita bread "pockets" to hold sandwich fillings

GRILLED CORN GF

Ingredients:
Fresh ears of corn, husks on • Butter • Salt

Directions:

1. With the husks on, soak ears of corn in water for 15 minutes.

2. Place the corn directly on the grill, rotating the ears with tongs as they cook for 10 to 15 minutes, depending on how hot the coals are.

3. Remove from the heat and peel carefully.

4. Butter and salt to enhance the flavor.

WATERMELON BOWL GF

Ingredients:
Watermelon, cut in half • Fresh fruit, cut into bite size chunks • Optional: a squeeze of lemon juice

Directions:

1. Hollow out the half-watermelon.

2. Scoop the fruit salad into the watermelon bowl. If you like, you can slide some pieces of fruit onto skewers and arrange the kabobs to come out of the watermelon bowl.

3. If your fruit salad includes apple slices or other fruit that risks turning brown in the sun, add a squirt of lemon juice to preserve color and freshness!

BURGERS WITH A TWIST

Ingredients:
1 egg, beaten
½ cup breadcrumbs
¾ cup shredded cheddar cheese
3 green onions, chopped
2 tablespoons Worcestershire sauce
1 tablespoon mustard
Dash pepper
1¼ pounds ground beef

Directions:
1. Combine the egg, breadcrumbs, cheese, green onions, Worcestershire sauce, mustard, and pepper.

2. Add the ground beef and mix. Shape into four patties.

3. Grill over direct heat.

4. Serve on toasted buns.

MY STORY

"Our family tries to picnic 'green,' that is, in an environmentally-friendly way. Sometimes we bike to our picnic spot rather than drive; other times we use cloth napkins and plates and silverware that we take back home. We always pack food in re-usable containers rather than plastic bags and we fill our own water bottles before we leave so we don't throw away plastic bottles. Our goal is to combine enjoying the outdoors with respecting the environment."

—*Serena, mother of four*

WALDORF SALAD GF

Ingredients:
2 to 3 cups chopped apple
1 cup cheddar cheese chunks
1 cup seedless grapes
½ cup diced celery
½ cup chopped walnuts
½ cup raisins
⅓ cup mayonnaise
2 teaspoons sugar
dash allspice
1 tablespoon lemon juice

Directions:
1. In a large bowl, mix the apple, cheese, grapes, celery, walnuts and raisins.

2. Combine the mayonnaise, sugar, allspice, and lemon juice; add to the apple mixture, stirring well.

3. Keep cold until ready to serve.

MULTI-GENERATIONAL FUN WITH FOOD

Grandparents don't mind if kids play with their food, so let them take part in the fun!

EDIBLE TINKERTOYS

Ingredients:
Bag of thin pretzel sticks
Bag of large marshmallows

Directions:

Skewer the marshmallows with the pretzel sticks as if you were playing with TinkerToys. Create houses, barns, boats, or anything you can think of! (Add gummy animals or animal crackers to inhabit your structures!)

Snack Ideas for Gamers

Gamers can work up quite an appetite so you'll want to have snacks available. You won't, however, want to put out anything that is likely to result in greasy hands or spills on controllers. Offer drinks in cans or boxes rather than glasses to minimize potential damage by enthusiastic players. Think neat finger foods, easy to grab between rounds.

Put out bowls of:

- Apple slices

- Pretzels

- Grapes

- Dry cereal like Kix, Fruit Loops, or Cheerios

- Yogurt or chocolate covered raisins

- Baby carrots

- Walnuts, pecans, or other less-greasy nuts

Popcorn Recipes

Looking for something a little more exotic in the popcorn department? Try these unusual takes on the traditional theater treat for family movie night!

ZESTY POPCORN

Ingredients:

   5 cups popcorn (popped)
   5 teaspoons butter, melted
   1 teaspoon Italian seasoning
   ¼ teaspoon garlic salt
   3 tablespoons grated Romano or Parmesan cheese

Directions:

1. Put the popcorn in a large serving bowl and set aside.

2. Stir together the butter, Italian seasoning and garlic salt.

3. Pour the butter mixture over the popcorn and mix well.

4. Sprinkle with cheese and mix again.

KETTLE CORN (GF)

Ingredients:
- ¼ cup vegetable oil or coconut oil
- ¼ cup white sugar
- ½ cup unpopped popcorn kernels
- ¼ tsp salt (optional)

Directions:
1. Heat the vegetable oil in a large pot over medium heat.

2. Once the oil is hot, stir in the popcorn and the sugar.

3. Cover the pot and shake it continuously so that the popcorn and sugar don't burn.

4. As soon as the popping has slowed down (if you can count to three between pops), take the pot off the stove and shake until the popping has stopped completely.

5. Dump the popcorn into a large bowl, sprinkle with salt, and let it cool. Break up any clusters with a plastic spoon.

For extra fun, add a little food coloring before popping!

CARAMEL CORN GF

Ingredients:
- 1½ gallons popcorn (popped)
- 2 cups brown sugar
- 1 cup butter
- ½ cup corn syrup (you can substitute honey or maple syrup)
- ½ teaspoon baking soda
- ½ teaspoon salt
- 1 teaspoon vanilla
- 1½ cups peanuts

Directions:
1. Preheat oven to 250 degrees.

2. In a medium-size pan, bring brown sugar, butter and corn syrup to a boil.

3. Boil gently for 5 minutes without stirring.

4. Remove the pan from the stove and add the baking soda, salt, vanilla, and peanuts.

5. Pour over the popcorn and mix until popcorn is coated.

6. Spread the popcorn on greased cookie sheets and bake for 1 hour, stirring every 15 to 20 minutes.

Cheap Eats

Having a Thrifty Family Fun Night? You can put together a delicious dinner using food you already have in the refrigerator and the pantry. Here are three budget-friendly recipes sure to please your brood.

MIX-IT-IN MAC AND CHEESE

Let each member of the family tweak a bowl of mac and cheese to suit his or her taste buds.

Ingredients:
1 lb. cooked macaroni
Milk, to taste
Butter, to taste
Variety of shredded cheese
Chopped, cooked broccoli
Chopped onions
Chopped mushrooms
Diced peppers
Cooked peas
Ground beef, cooked and crumbled
Bacon bits
Hot dogs, cooked and chopped

Directions:
1. To the cooked macaroni, add milk and butter to achieve the desired consistency. (Or use a packaged mix, if desired.)

2. Set out the other ingredients in separate bowls for add-ins. Let everyone scoop out a bowl of macaroni and add any extras that look appealing!

STIR-FRY DINNER

This flexible stir-fry recipe uses up the leftovers in the fridge, making use of whatever you have on hand and requiring few, if any, extra purchases at the grocery store.

Ingredients:

2 tablespoons olive oil, divided
1 pound meat or meat substitute (choose one or more from list below)
1 onion, chopped
1 clove garlic, minced
1 teaspoon ginger
4 cups vegetables (choose three or more from list below)
½ cup broth (chicken, beef, or vegetable)
2 tablespoons soy sauce
2 teaspoons cornstarch
½ cup extra ingredient (choose one from list below)

Meat choices: boneless chicken strips, boneless beef stir-fry strips, boneless pork strips, raw shrimp, tofu cubes

Vegetable choices: pepper strips, mushroom slices, celery pieces, snow peas, zucchini slices, carrot slices, broccoli florets

Extra ingredients: nuts, sesame seeds, crispy Chinese noodles, crispy fried onion bits

Directions:

1. Heat 1 tablespoon of oil over high heat. Add meat and stir-fry until just cooked through. Set meat aside.

2. Heat remaining tablespoon of oil in pan; add onion, garlic, and ginger. Cook for 1 minute. Add vegetable choices and cook for another 2 minutes.

3. Add the broth to the vegetables, cover, and let steam for 2 or 3 minutes.

4. Meanwhile, in a small bowl, stir together soy sauce and corn-starch.

5. When vegetables are tender, add the meat and soy sauce mix-ture to the pan. Stir-fry for another 1 to 2 minutes or until the sauce is thickened.

6. Remove from heat and sprinkle with the extra ingredient. Serve over rice.

MAKE-YOUR-OWN ICE CREAM GF

Each person in the family can make his or her very own ice cream—in a bag! The only thing you may need to buy is half-and-half.

Ingredients (for a single serving):
2 tablespoons sugar
1 cup half and half
½ tsp vanilla

Additional supplies needed:
½ cup of salt
Ice cubes
Small and large re-sealable plastic bags

Directions:
1. Fill the large plastic bag halfway with ice cubes; add ½ cup of salt.

2. Fill the smaller bag with sugar, half-and-half, and vanilla. Seal it shut and place it inside the larger bag, then seal the larger bag.

3. Shake the bag until the mixture hardens (about 5 minutes).

4. Dump the ice cream from the small bag into a bowl and enjoy!

Cooking for Card Sharks

You'll want to make bite-size goodies for kids who are trying to grasp a handful of cards and nibble at the same time. The first two recipes resemble traditional hot dogs and hamburgers, but with a fun twist. The third is a variation on the ever-popular kid's meal: chicken fingers. The last recipe will appeal to those looking for a healthier alternative. All are easy enough for the kids to make with minimal help from an adult. Add a communal plate of celery and carrot sticks to round out the meal.

TIP

For kids, it's often the name that counts. Would they eat celery with peanut butter and raisins if it wasn't called Ants on a Log? In addition to experimenting with new recipes, try re-naming tried-and-true dishes to see if you can generate some interest in mealtime.

ROADKILL BURGERS

Ingredients:
1 pound ground beef
1 ½ cups shredded cheddar cheese
1 6-ounce can French fried onions
2 cans crescent rolls

Directions:
1. Brown ground beef; drain fat.

2. Mix cheese and onions into the ground beef.

3. Place a spoonful of the beef mixture onto a crescent roll and fold it over to seal in the filling. Repeat with rest of rolls and meat.

4. Place burgers on ungreased cookie sheet. Bake at 350 degrees for about 8 minutes or until light brown.

FOWL FINGERS

Ingredients:
1 6-ounce can French fried onions
¼ cup flour
2 pounds boneless chicken tenders
2 large eggs, beaten

Directions:
1. Put the fried onions and flour together in a large, re-sealable plastic bag.

2. With a rolling pin, crush the fried onions inside the bag. Dump the contents onto a plate.

3. Dip the chicken pieces into the beaten egg, then coat in the onion and flour mixture.

4. Bake at 400 degrees for 15 minutes.

Serve with fun dipping sauces like honey mustard or spicy buffalo ranch.

PIGGIES IN A BLANKET

Ingredients:
1 package of mini hot dogs
1 can crescent rolls

Directions:

1. Unroll the dough and separate it along the perforations. Cut each dough triangle into thirds.

2. Roll each piece of dough around one mini hot dog. Repeat with remainder of dough.

3. Bake at 350 degrees on ungreased cookie sheet for about 12 minutes or until light brown.

Serve with your favorite dipping sauce for the "piggies," like honey mustard.

HUNGRY HUNGRY HUMMUS GF

Ingredients:
1 15-ounce can chickpeas, rinsed and drained
1 tablespoon chopped garlic
¼ cup olive oil
3 tablespoons lemon juice
2 tablespoons tahini
1 teaspoon ground cumin
½ teaspoon salt
⅛ teaspoon cayenne pepper
¼ teaspoon paprika

Directions:
1. Puree all ingredients in a food processor until smooth; add a tablespoon of water if necessary for desired consistency.

2. Serve with pita bread triangles or pita chips, pretzels, or raw veggies.

TRADITIONAL BOARD GAME NIGHT

Board games have seen a resurgence recently as families re-discover old favorites as well as embrace the newest game crazes. Even though board games have been around for about 7,000 years (the very first games were two-player games like Mancala and chess), board games caught on as a family activity after World War II, with Monopoly, Scrabble, and Parcheesi® topping the list of favorites. Not long after, games especially for children, like Candyland and Shoots and Ladders, were introduced.

Trivial Pursuit® reignited interest in board games when it burst onto the scene in the 1980s, and sillier games like Pictionary, Heads Up, and iMAgiNiff ® followed. Recently, technology has infiltrated the board game industry, and many games now include a digital component.

TIDBIT

Mass-produced board games first appeared in the U.S. in the 1840s and were intended to encourage Christian virtue and principles by rewarding the "right" moves and punishing the "wrong" ones. It wasn't until later that century that Milton Bradley and George S. Parker steered the game industry in a new direction, creating games to be played for fun rather than as a teaching tool.

Even traditional games have been updated and re-imagined to be more relevant and appealing for today's players. Monopoly players can now use credit cards, and play with tokens like jets and flat-screen TVs. A new version of Clue has a feature that allows players to text and has a black light that helps with finding clues. New versions of Sorry® and Scrabble® aimed at today's busy families are designed to last about 20 minutes rather than a few hours.

TIDBIT

Although Charles Darrow gets the credit for bringing the game of Monopoly to the attention of Parker Brothers, many believe that Elizabeth Magie created the original to demonstrate the way landlords abused their tenants. Darrow discovered her game in the early 1930s and changed the locations to familiar places in Atlantic City. The first time he tried to sell it to Parker Brothers, the company rejected it on the basis that it was too complicated. But, like a lot of folks during the Great Depression, Darrow was unemployed and he believed that a game allowing people to amass property and wealth would be a welcome escape from real life. After selling 5,000 games that he made himself, he approached Parker Brothers again. This time the executives were interested. That was a good decision on the part of the company, as 750 million people have played the game since it came on the market in the mid-1930s.

TIDBIT

In 1931, an out-of-work architect decided to invent a game that was based half on luck and half on skill. After much deliberation, he came up with the idea of Scrabble. He couldn't interest any toy companies in the game, and so for a number of years, he made the games himself for family and friends. He met a man named James Bruno in 1948 who loved the Scrabble idea; Bruno bought the rights and began making games in an abandoned schoolhouse in Connecticut. After losing money for four straight years, he had a bit of luck. Jack Strauss, the chairman of Macy's, the world's largest department store, discovered the game while on vacation in 1952 and ordered some for his store. Today, the game is found in one out of every three American homes and it is sold in 121 countries, making it the world's best-selling word game.

What makes a great board game?

Popular board games may seem to have little in common with one another, but all share several traits that make them stand out.

To begin with, the best games challenge experienced players but are simple enough for new players to enjoy. No one is bored, and no one is frustrated. In addition, rules are not overly complicated, the game moves along at a comfortable pace, and the length of time it takes to play is well suited for the recommended age range.

Top games are also flexible when it comes to number of players; the "fun factor" of these games isn't affected by adding or subtracting players. Also, the best games don't leave anyone out for a significant stretch of time (think musical chairs).

You might not even realize it, but the best games also teach something—trivia facts, money management, or skills like adding or spelling. In addition to inherent educational value, a good game is different each time it's played, making it fun to play over and over again.

Finally, the classic versions of popular games stand up to the test of time. While new versions that pull in pop culture or appeal to tech-savvy teens may be introduced, the original games are still tops.

Classic Family Board Games

Of the thousands of games on the market today, only a handful are considered classics: popular, timeless games that your children will likely be playing with their own children someday. Has your family played them all?

BOGGLE®: Using a grid of lettered dice, players must find words in sequences of adjacent letters.

CANDYLAND®: This is often one of the first games kids learn how to play because only color matching and minimal counting are required. Players race around the board to find the lost King of Candyland.

CHECKERS®: This simple game offers a surprising range of possibilities. Even though it's known as a two-player game, teams can play also, with a leader making the final decision about each move. Your family might also decide to have two or three games going at once, trading players after each round.

CHUTES AND LADDERS®: Players advance pieces according to a spinner, climbing ladders and heading down chutes. Like many old board games, this one offers a lesson in morality; actions have consequences, both good and bad!

CLUE®: This clue-based mystery game encourages players to use their problem-solving and reasoning skills to solve a murder. A number of versions are available for different age groups.

THE GAME OF LIFE®: Intended for ages nine and up, Life® allows players to manage a mortgage, career choices, insurance, and the unexpected twists and turns of life. A player's choices determine how the game will progress.

JENGA®: Players slide vertically stacked game pieces out one by one; the person who makes the tower fall over loses. Anyone can play—the only skill required is a steady hand!

MONOPOLY®: Future real estate tycoons ages eight and up will love to amass, trade, and upgrade property. With dozens of pop culture versions, Monopoly can teach kids about bargaining and investing.

PARCHEESI®: Known as a "cross and circle" game with a number of variations played around the world, Parcheesi requires two to four players to move their pawns around the board in a race to the center.

PICTIONARY®: Players must draw clues so that their teammates can guess what is written on the chosen card, allowing the team to move ahead on the game board. Artistic skills are not required; often the concept can be conveyed with a clever stick figure or simple sketch. The original game is for ages 12 and up, but there is a junior version available with easier words for younger players. This is a great game for a large group if you set up an easel for drawing.

TIP

Try to come up with your own unique twist to a favorite board game! Pictionary, for instance, can be changed so that every turn is a battle between teams, like an "all play." Or you can challenge the artists by making them draw blindfolded or by poking a pencil through a wrapping paper tube and having a person hold each end as they work together to draw a picture! Be creative!

SCRABBLE®: A word game for two to four players, Scrabble lets competitors expand their knowledge of vocabulary within an exciting and challenging format. Players score points by using lettered tiles to form words across and down the game board, like a crossword puzzle.

SORRY®: Younger players appreciate the simplicity of this game, while older, more experienced players can concoct strategies to trade places and block opponents. No player, however, will be able to get through the game without saying, "Sorry!"

TRIVIAL PURSUIT®: The ultimate trivia game, Trivial Pursuit challenges players to remember facts involving literature, history, sports, and other topics as they try to add plastic subject-area pieces to fill a "pie." Check out the kids' version of this game for ages eight and up or the special editions in a variety of subject areas.

TROUBLE®: The pop-o-matic bubble that holds the die is the most memorable feature of this game! Players race four pieces around a board, hoping to land on an opponent's piece to send it back to the start.

YAHTZEE®: Success in this simple game hinges on a roll of the dice, but the multiple point combinations reinforce math skills, statistics, and other lessons.

Some Terrific Games You May Not Know About

As delightful as the classics are, don't discount the excellent games available that are not as well known. It can be great fun to "discover" a new game—or to rediscover one you played as a child! Whether your family likes games of strategy, skill, or luck, you'll find a new favorite from among those in our list.

APPLES TO APPLES®: With a junior version available for kids under 12 as well as the original for adults, this word-association game requires players to make matches with the nouns and adjectives in the deck of cards. The results are often hilarious!

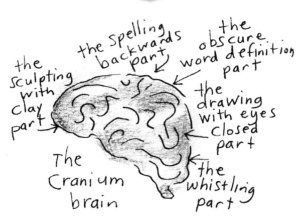

the spelling backwards part

the obscure word definition part

the sculpting with clay part

the drawing with eyes closed part

The Cranium brain

the whistling part

CRANIUM®: Everyone has a chance to shine in Cranium! Billed as "The Game for Your Whole Brain," Cranium involves teams moving around a board as they complete in various activities such as drawing, sculpting, spelling, answering trivia questions, playing charades, or humming. Special editions include Cadoo® for kids and Cranium: The Family Fun Game®.

FLUXX®: Deceptively simple, Fluxx is a fast-paced game that can be played with as few as 2 players or as many as half a dozen, making it great for families. Based on what cards are drawn and played, the rules constantly change—including how to win the game! Because luck (rather than skill) plays such a large role, everyone in the family has an equal chance of winning! Check out the themed Fluxx editions, like Monty Python Fluxx® and Zombie Fluxx®.

HEADS UP®: Ellen DeGeneres popularized this hilarious game on her TV show! Put on a headband, slip cards onto the front without looking at them, and try to guess what's written on the cards based on your teammates' clues. Sound easy? How would your teammates act out "changing a diaper" or "getting married?" (Also available as an app.)

IMAGINIFF®: Do you ever wonder what your family members really think of you? If you were an article of clothing, would they say you were a pair of jeans, a bathrobe, or a ball gown? What if you were a theme park ride? Would you be the bumper cars, a merry-go-round, or a roller coaster? You get the idea! Everyone votes and the most popular answer wins. Up to eight people can play, so it's great for a large family.

KERPLUNK®: Parents might remember this game, which was introduced in the '60s. Straws criss-cross through holes in a plastic tube; marbles are placed on top of the "web" created by the straws. Players take turns removing a straw, trying to prevent marbles from falling out of a hole at the base of the tube. The player who allows the fewest number of marbles to drop wins the game.

TIDBIT

If your family lived in Europe, you might participate in the unlikely yet fascinating sport known as chess-boxing. Players alternate between four minutes of chess playing and two minutes of boxing. The game is over when there is a checkmate or a knockout.

TIP

To avoid breaking the bank, trade board games with other families. Or invite another family over on game night and ask them to bring some of their favorite games!

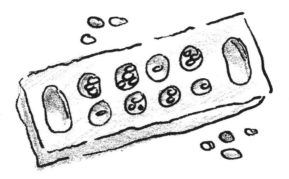

MANCALA: This game of African origin is described as simple to learn and difficult to master, making it suitable for players with a wide range of abilities. Essentially, players must capture as many stones as possible.

MASTERPIECE®: This art auction game is best suited for older kids as the pace might be a bit slow for the littler ones. Strategy and luck combine for moments of excitement and suspense as players discover the value of paintings bought at an "auction": A piece of art might be worth three times what you paid for it, or it might be a worthless fraud! Kids will get a little art history lesson as they learn to recognize classic paintings included with the game.

MUNCHKIN®: Compete to slay monsters and abscond with magic items, working your way from level 1 to level 10! This award-winning card game is fast-paced and silly (and rated PG, with crude humor best suited for pre-teens and up). Spoofing Dungeons and Dragons®, Munchkin travels easily for on-the-go fun.

TIP

If you're playing a game for the first time, have a tried-and-true stand-by in case your family isn't crazy about the new one.

QUIDDLER®: A fast and easy game for kids who know how to read, Quiddler requires players to create words from the lettered cards in their hands. Players try to use the letters with the highest point values. Bonuses are awarded to players who make the most words and the longest word in each round. Games last from 20 to 40 minutes.

QWITCH®: Three to five players race to play cards in sequence in this exciting, "quick switch" game. As letters and numbers go up, down, or remain the same, each player tries to get rid of all of his cards to win. Kids over seven will enjoy this one!

RAT-A-TAT CAT®: A delightful (and delightfully simple) numbers game, Rat-a-Tat Cat boasts charming illustrations on its deck of cards that kids will love. Essentially, each player tries to be the one holding four cards with the lowest total value at the game's end. Warning: The "swap" cards have a way of throwing off everyone's game plan!

SAY ANYTHING FAMILY®: Which celebrity would make the worst babysitter? What magical power would be the coolest to have? There are no right or wrong answers, just a lot of strong opinions! Players try to figure out which answer the judge of a given round will like best. Winner of dozens of awards, Say Anything is easy to play and great for families with kids over 8 who really want to get to know each other better!

SET®: This challenging "family game of visual perception" has won 25 best game awards, including honors from MENSA, Parents Magazine, and Games Magazine. To begin, twelve or fifteen cards from the Set deck are placed face up, with each card identified by four features (color, number, shape, shading). Players try to identify as many "sets" as possible (a "set" is a group of three cards in which each feature is either the same or different). Younger players are often better at seeing sets than adults!

SLAMWICH®: This award-winning game rewards those with fast hands and sharp eyes, two areas where kids have an advantage over parents! Players will flip, stack, and slap this "loaf" of cards to build slamwiches, each trying to collect as many cards as possible. Slamwich helps teach skills such as visual discrimination and sequencing.

SLEEPING QUEENS®: Unable to fall asleep one night, 6-year old Miranda Evarts imagined a game in which she saved colorful queens who'd fallen under a sleeping spell. In the months that followed, Miranda's family helped her develop rules for the game and they eventually joined forces with the award-winning game company Gamewright to produce Sleeping Queens. With strategy, simple arithmetic, and a bit of luck, players compete to wake up the most queens – but beware poisonous potions and dangerous dragons!

STONE SOUP®: In this game based on the popular folk-tale-turned-children's-book, players take turns adding food cards to the "pot" following a certain sequence of ingredients. Like the card game "Liar, Liar" (see page 176), a player may be forced to bluff by adding the wrong card if she doesn't have the one that's needed. You might be surprised at how well your kids can fib!

STORY CUBES ® : Create your own stories, create your own rules! Roll a handful of dice with pictures on each face and then take turns making up a story based on the images—or collaborate on a story. Tweak the rules to fit your family by adding time limits or awarding points for the most dice used in one story. Add extra sets of story cubes for even more game options.

TELESTRATIONS®: Imagine if the ages-old party game Telephone had a drawing component: that's Telestrations! As erasable sketchbooks are passed around the family circle, players are guessing what words the others are trying to illustrate, then drawing their responses. In the last round, the initial words are revealed, along with everyone's guesses (that get wilder and more off track as the sketchbooks make their way through the group), culminating in the reveal of the final, unpredictable guess.

XACTICA®: The game's slogan is "Beware the Last Card" because of the precision required as players try to predict exactly the outcome of playing eight cards. An innovative version of the popular card game Spades, Xactica is somewhat challenging to learn; there are many rules to game play, but once mastered it's great fun. Families with kids ages 12 and up will enjoy it.

TIDBIT

The spots on dice are called pips!

Creating Your Own Special Family Game

Involve the whole family in creating a game of your very own. You can make an entirely original game or you can alter a favorite game so it has special meaning for your family.

You might start with a board game you already have and talk about how you could change the rules or add or subtract various pieces. Or visit a yard sale and buy several used games; use pieces from each to create a whole new game with a new set of rules. Think big: How about supersizing a game like Checkers? You can paint a checkerboard pattern on a plastic sheet or a large piece of cardboard.

MY STORY

"We play a game called **Penny Face.** Ahead of time, we make a game card for each player by drawing a face made up of penny-size circles. The winner is the one who fills up his or her face first with pennies. We place a pile of pennies and a deck of cards in the middle of the table. Each person takes turns drawing a card. The cards are valued this way: for an Ace, add two pennies to your face; for a King, Queen, or Jack, add one penny to your face; for sevens, take one penny off of your face and add it to the face of another player; for threes, take one penny away from the face of another player and add it to yours. If you get the five of diamonds, you have to wipe all the pennies off of your face and start again! Other cards have no value. We love our game!"

—*Colleen, mother of four*

You can also make a unique game from scratch. Think about the kind of games your family likes to play. Do the kids prefer games of luck, strategy, or some combination of the two? Sketch out a rough game board and discuss what the rules should be. It helps to think about what you like and don't like about other games you've played. Study the directions of classic games. You can start with a simple premise of rolling dice and moving game pieces, then add twists and turns to make the game more interesting. Perhaps your game involves your family going on vacation, or getting from home to the zoo. Invent obstacles you might encounter along the way, like a mean dog or nasty neighbor. It's likely that you'll tweak the rules the first few times you play.

MY STORY

"We play a sort of puzzle game that requires a little preparation. We take song lyrics, proverbs, or pictures from magazines—one item per person—and paste them on pieces of cardboard. Then we cut up each one into at least four pieces. Each person is given one piece of one item, and the others are placed on the table upside down. One at a time, each player turns over a piece to see if it matches the piece he has. If it does, he places it face up on the table; if not, he puts it back. The first one to recreate his song, proverb or magazine picture is the winner."

—*Latonya, mother of three*

If you have an old game board (or can find one at a thrift store or tag sale), you can glue the new game you've designed over the old game. Otherwise, use a piece of white foam board: It's sturdy but lightweight. Be creative with your game board! Use photos of your child's school, favorite restaurant, playground, or even friends and family members. You can also cut out items from magazines that have meaning to you and your kids. For the "start" square, use a photo of your house. Stamps and stickers will make decorating easy. Craft stores sell products that will seal the board once you've finished it to protect it from use. Your kids can come up with clever little items

TIDBIT

If you think you've created a game other families would enjoy, contact a company that manufactures games and describe your idea. The game Sleeping Queens®, sold by Gamewright, was invented by six-year-old Miranda Evarts on a March night in 2003 as she was trying to fall asleep. She imagined a slew of silly queens who needed to be awakened. Miranda and her sister, who are homeschooled, worked with their friends and parents to develop her idea into a working game.

Gamewright receives several hundred ideas every year for new games and accepts about half a dozen of them. According to company executives, the best way to create a top-notch game is to invite friends over to play it with you and offer feedback. Sleeping Queens is Gamewright's first kid-invented game. A helpful book on the topic is *The Game Inventor's Guidebook: How to Invent and Sell Board Games, Card Games, Role-Playing Games, & Everything in Between!* By Brian Tinsman (Morgan James Publishing, 2008).

to serve as game tokens, and you can buy dice and cards at a local dollar store. If you need cards other than traditional playing cards, use a pack of index cards or blank place cards to make your own.

Some game manufacturers offer families a way to create their own games based on classics, like Monopoly. Make-your-own-opoly, for instance, allows families to customize a Monopoly game board, cards, play money, and moving pieces with a PC and a color printer. Easy to follow instructions and software will guide you as you create your unique property trading game. A website for Ready-Made Game Boards allows you to download templates to create educational games. Your family can choose clip-art or photos to personalize the game.

Visit our website for more information about these creative products. If your family wants to explore game-making further, read *The Kobold Guide to Board Game Design* by Mike Selinker et al (Open Design, 2011).

Television game shows are another great inspiration for family games. Play your own version of Wheel of Fortune, for instance. Set up an easel and white board or oversized pad of paper. One person at a time thinks of a phrase, puts blanks representing each letter on the board, and gives a general category like "occupation" or "something found in the kitchen." Each person can guess one letter and, if that letter is in the phrase, take one guess at what the word might be. Think about the game shows your family likes to watch and invent a game based on your favorites!

CHAPTER EIGHT

A CHARITABLE FAMILY FUN NIGHT

Volunteering together will strengthen your family bonds in a way that is not only fun, but also fulfilling. By volunteering as a family, you can convey to your kids how much they matter—not just to you, but also to the greater community and even to the world. Laying the groundwork for community service pays off: Studies show that people who volunteer when they are young are significantly more likely to volunteer as adults.

For older kids, the concept of a Family Fun Night will be even more appealing if community service is involved. Teens like taking part in real-world activities and feel a genuine sense of satisfaction from helping others. With adult supervision, small children can be valuable helpers, too. According to government surveys, young families and those with older children volunteer at about the same rate.

There are all sorts of ways your family can help out on a regular basis in your area, from participating in events with established organizations to creating opportunities to help people you know.

Tips for Family Volunteering

To ensure that your experience is a positive one, take these ideas and strategies into consideration:

1. Match the volunteer opportunity to your family's interests. As a group, brainstorm ideas for helping out.

2. Find a way to help where children are an integral part of the experience, not just relegated to observing or menial jobs. This involves finding out exactly how volunteers are put to use in a given agency.

3. Ask what type of preparation or training is provided for volunteers.

4. Don't over commit at first. You don't have to take on something overwhelming to serve. Find out exactly what will be expected of you. Start small and increase your participation if your family agrees that it would be the right thing for everyone.

TIP

Consider taking part in National Family Volunteer Day, held each year on the Saturday before Thanksgiving and sponsored by the Points of Light Foundation and Volunteer Center National Network. This day of service was designed to highlight the benefits of family volunteering and to showcase the opportunities available for families wishing to help out in their communities. Families can take part in a variety of community service projects across the country, from park clean-ups to playground building. For more information about this event (and about a similar one for young people called Global Youth Service Day), check out www.FamilyFunNight.org!

5. Be willing to try again if the first situation isn't right for you. Assess what was less than desirable and come up with some other possibilities.

6. Treat it as a job: Show up ready to work and on time. Encourage the kids to step up whenever they notice something needs to be done.

7. Keeping tip #6 in mind, have fun. Let the kids see that you enjoy helping out.

8. Have a family debriefing session when it's all over. Reflect on the experience and ask how everyone felt about it.

How and where to help

To find a great volunteer opportunity near you, check out local and regional newspapers or community bulletin boards at stores or places of worship. If you don't find anything suitable, visit your town's website. Most states also support websites that list specific volunteer

10 THINGS YOUR KIDS WILL GET FROM VOLUNTEERING WITH YOU

1. A greater sense of their role and responsibilities in the community

2. The message that one person can indeed make a difference for the better

3. The satisfaction of realizing that being on the giving end can feel better than being on the taking end

4. A lesson in empathy, respect, and tolerance. Many of the families lining up to eat in a soup kitchen don't look that different from our own families.

5. Confidence as they contribute in an adult world

6. Skills they may need in a job someday

7. A sense of empowerment from helping others

8. Greater respect for you, their parents

9. New friends, many of whom will be great role models

10. The opportunity to represent their peers in a positive way

opportunities. The Volunteer Center of Rhode Island's site, for instance, displays over 100 family-friendly postings from agencies statewide. It's important for families to be assertive as they look for ways to serve: One survey reported that even though nearly three-quarters of agencies would be interested in involving family volunteers, 83 percent do not actively recruit them.

MY STORY

"Every year, our family holds a Box Meal Auction. We invite our friends and neighbors to come and bring a gourmet box lunch (or dinner), wrapped up neatly. Then we auction off each box (with the rule that no one can buy back her own meal). The money we earn goes to fund cancer research."

—*Sarah, mother of four*

Ideas for getting involved with an established organization

Some families prefer to sign on with an organization that is already active in the area. Perhaps one of the following suggestions will inspire you.

- Sign up for a weekly shift at your local community kitchen. You can cook, serve, or clean up afterward. Usually you will have a time when you can sit and eat with your family and the other volunteers. It's a powerful reminder to your kids about your family's blessings.

- If your family loves animals, check with your local animal shelter to see if you can help out. You might be asked to collect old blankets and towels for the animal cages. Often they need volunteers to walk the dogs (and kids usually are required to have parental supervision), making it the perfect family activity.

TIDBIT

Nearly 98 percent of the agencies that used family volunteers found it to be a very effective way to deliver services to those in need, with over 98 percent reporting that families benefitted above and beyond the volunteer experience alone.

- Deliver Meals on Wheels to seniors in your community.

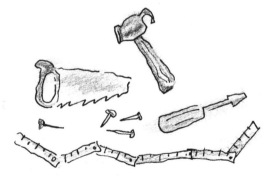

- Do you have a local theater that uses volunteer ushers? Sign up as a group and after you've finished showing patrons to their seats, you can enjoy the performance—usually for free!

- Explore the needs of your local community youth or recreation center, Boys and Girls Club, or YMCA. Perhaps your family can assist at the indoor climbing wall, belaying climbers or helping them get into their harnesses. Or you can offer to lead a group on one your favorite family hikes.

- From donating blood to helping in times of disaster, the Red Cross has a wide range of needs that families with older kids can help meet. The Red Cross welcomes youth participation, and trains young people to become involved in community disaster education, preparation, and response through the youth disaster corps.

- Contact your local DCYF (Department of Children, Youth, and Families) office and ask how you can help the area's foster children. Perhaps you and your kids can donate items in need or decorate duffel bags for kids who move frequently and have no way to carry their things.

- You and your older kids can work with Habitat for Humanity, a nonprofit ministry that builds affordable houses for people in need.

- Is there a cause you believe in as a family? Are you concerned about the rights of children around the world? Contact an organization like UNICEF and find out how you can help. Would you like to focus your attention on eradicating world hunger? Consider organizing a family fund-raiser for Heifer International: For a minimal amount of money, you can give a poor family in another part of the world a flock of chicks or a sheep or goat. How about dogs and cats waiting in shelters? In just a few minutes, you can use social media to help a rescue organization spread the word about animals available for adoption. There are as many ways to help as causes to support!

TIDBIT

According to a government survey, about 37 percent of families actively volunteer together. Family volunteering tends to become a tradition once it's been established, with 80 percent of those interviewed continuing to volunteer with relatives.

Ideas for creating your own volunteer opportunities

There are a number of things your family can do on its own to serve those in need who live around the corner as well as around the world.

- Take an evening to write letters to teachers who inspired you, or to congressmen and women or other people in positions of power to express your family's opinion about an issue of importance to all of you.

- Give a single parent a free night: Invite her kids over to spend the evening with you playing family games!

- Pick up trash at a local park or along a walking path (just remember your disposable gloves).

- Offer to help an elderly neighbor by raking leaves, walking his dog, shoveling the driveway, or teaching him to use a computer or navigate the Internet.

- Does your family have talent? Entertain seniors at a nursing home or community center with your musical (or other) talents.

- Bake cookies and deliver them to the fire department or to a local senior center.

• Make fleece blankets and donate them to soldiers overseas.

• "Adopt" a family living at a homeless shelter and treat the children to a weekly movie, dinner out, or local sporting event.

• A family can coach a team: While the parents direct the action on the field, kids can help by keeping score, organizing equipment, and handing out drinks or snacks.

• As a family, mentor a child in need. Invite her to do dinner, help her with homework and other school projects, and include her in sporting activities.

• Adopt a playground: Plant flowers, fix broken equipment, and paint benches.

- Computer savvy families can offer to manage the website for a non-profit organization or place of worship.

- Ask your local fire department if they'd like you to re-paint any of the hydrants.

- Artistic families can paint a mural on a community center wall, in a Sunday school room, or on the side of a municipal building (maybe one that will cover graffiti!).

- Offer to bring your (well-behaved) dog to the children's section of your public library so that children who struggle with reading can make strides reading aloud to your attentive pet.

- Have a yard sale and donate all of the money to a charity that has special meaning for your family.

TIP

To make cozy blankets you can donate, buy 1½ yards of fleece and another 1 ½ yards of fleece in a different, but complementary, pattern and color. Lay one piece on top of the other, with the right sides facing out, and cut a 3-inch long fringe along each side of the doubled-up material. Cut a 3-inch square out of each corner. Assign one family member to each side of the blanket; you will attach the two pieces of fleece together by tying (with a double knot) the top piece of fringe to the one underneath.

CHAPTER NINE

MULTI-GENERATIONAL FAMILY FUN NIGHT

There are a number of wonderful activities for grandparents, parents, and children to do together that everyone will love. The key is to identify activities that truly are fun for all, where everyone is engaged: No antique stores or cartoon marathons allowed!

Reading Aloud

Reading books aloud to your children or grandchildren is a simple ritual that will help them establish a positive and lasting relationship with literature. When you read to kids, even for just 15 minutes at a time, you are helping to improve their vocabulary, inspire their imaginations, and enhance their listening skills.

Always begin by introducing the book: Read the title, subtitle, and the author's name. Mention any information that you think is important for an understanding of the story, and indicate the reasons you chose the book. You can decide whether it's best to share facts about the author or about specific events in the story (such as whether it's based on a true story) before or after you've finished the book. A bit of information piques curiosity; too much information spoils the story!

TIP

When reading a book over the course of several weeks, always review what happened previously before you start reading again.

Read expressively with inflection and enthusiasm. Be animated! Allow your eyes and your voice to convey what's happening in the story. Pay close attention to what you're reading so that you know whether to raise or lower your voice, speed up or slow down, or speak in a higher or lower tone. Pause for dramatic effect. Differentiate among characters. All of these techniques help listeners engage in your story. If you read for more than about 20 minutes, allow the kids to ask questions or make comments as you go along. Also stop to explain words or ideas you think your kids might find confusing.

Children who are listening to a story might find their focus improves if they are involved in an activity such as drawing scenes they imagine from the book, playing with a stuffed animal (especially if the animal is represented in the story), knitting or crocheting, stacking blocks, or molding with Play-Doh.

After you finish reading, engage the family in a discussion of the book. Even the youngest members of the family will be able to make worthwhile contributions to a literary dialogue if you ask the right questions!

Here are some great book discussion topics:

The characters: What did you think of ___? What did you like about him or her? What didn't you like? What are some words you would use to describe him or her: Brave? Cruel? Kind? Loyal? Greedy? Why did the character do the things s/he did? Would you have done the same things? Is this person like anyone you know? If you could be best friends with anyone in the book, who would it be? Why?

The plot or events of the story: What was the most important thing that happened? What made that moment so important? What were you thinking when it happened? Did you expect it to happen or were you surprised? Was there anything you expected to happen that didn't?

MY STORY

"Beware of beloved books from your own youth! I thought my kids would love a book called *Half Magic* as much as I did when I was young, but the dialogue was too antiquated and the story didn't move along quickly enough for them. I remembered it so differently! Some classics still work for kids today (mine did love *Pippi Longstocking*), but my advice for parents and grandparents is to reassess them yourself before reading them to your kids."

—Mira, mother of two

The ending: How do you feel about the way the story ended? If you could re-write this book, would you change the ending? If you would, how would you change it? Did anything about the ending surprise you? By the time the story ended, who learned or changed the most? Did you learn anything? Would you be interested to know what happens to the characters after the story ended?

In conclusion... How would you describe this book to a friend? Would you want to read another book by the same author or about the same characters?

You may think that your child's listening level (which is different from his or her reading level) is the most important factor to consider when selecting a read-aloud book. As important as that is, your own enthusiasm for the book is just as critical! In fact, your child would likely be engaged in a story that is a bit above his level if you read it with passion. Don't sacrifice your own reading pleasure!

When making a selection, look for books with engaging, well-paced storylines, as well as elements of suspense and adventure. For younger kids, you may initially want to read two or three shorter books by the same author. This will give them a sense of that author's voice but won't require them to stay focused for weeks at a time while you work through a longer novel.

TIDBIT

The average reading speed is about 30 pages per hour. With this in mind, you can determine how long it will take to read a given book to your family.

You can opt for a non-fiction book if the entire family is interested in the topic: If, for example, you will be travelling to Ireland on your next vacation, you may be excited to learn about the country and its history. If you

will be visiting the planetarium in a few weeks, you might find an interesting book on astronomy.

Be aware that there is a difference between a great book and a great *read-aloud* book. Books that you remember being among your favorites when you were younger might not work well in the read-aloud format. In addition, books with lengthy sections of descriptive passages are not as interesting to listen to as those with a lot of action. Extensive passages of dialogue make a book less than ideal, and it can be confusing unless the reader consistently uses different voices for each character.

TIP

Some parents may remember watching Reading Rainbow, which debuted on PBS in 1983. In 2012, a Reading Rainbow App was released for the iPad that allows kids to read unlimited books, enjoy video field trips featuring LeVar Burton (the host of the original television show), and collect rewards for reading. Within a year and a half, the app boasted 10 million books read and videos watched!

You have access to great resources when you are choosing titles to read: your child's school librarian, your local public library's children's librarian, your child's teacher, and a number of read-aloud websites. Look for book bargains at your library's book sale, tag sales, used book stores, or book clubs through your children's schools. You can also trade books with other families.

For a list of great books, book series, and authors to inspire you and get you started—including recommendations by other parents and grandparents—check out our website.

You'll find that many family-friendly books have multiple references to food—some serious, some silly. It's always fun to plan a meal around the theme of a book you're reading together. Some books make it easy with companion cookbooks: *The Little House on the Prairie* series, for instance, includes a cookbook called *The Little House Cookbook* (by Barbara M. Walker) that features more than one hundred frontier recipes from the classic stories. If you're reading *Charlie and the Chocolate Factory* or *James and the Giant Peach*, check

MY STORY

"We established the 'two chapter rule' for books we read to the kids. Before giving a book I've chosen the thumbs down, the kids need to listen to at least two chapters. This gives them a bit of control, and yet forces them to give the book a chance before they reject it. So far, no vetoes! They have always wanted to hear more after the first two chapters."

—Mike, father of two

MY STORY

"We often start reading a book together, then finish it separately... one child might borrow it and read it for awhile, then pass it to another. Or we may do some reading to the younger kids while they're in the tub. The only rule is that when everyone has finished it, we all get together and discuss it."

—*Colleen, mother of five*

out Roald Dahl's *Revolting Recipes* (by Josie Fision and Felicity Dahl). Amy Cotler has written *The Secret Garden Cookbook: Recipes Inspired by Frances Hodgson Burnett's The Secret Garden*. For a comprehensive list of literature-inspired cookbooks, visit our website. If the book you're reading doesn't have a cookbook associated with it, go online and look for recipes that would complement the topic, historical period, or geographic location of your title.

MY STORY

"We formed a parent-child book club with other families in our neighborhood. We all read the same book aloud to our kids during the month and then get together for a discussion at someone's house. Knowing that we have that monthly meeting puts reading at the top of our priority list."

—*Selena, mother of three*

TIP

For very young kids who enjoy picture books, you can combine an activity with the book for a complete Family Fun Night: *A House Is a House for Me* (Mary Ann Hoberman) can inspire the kids to build their own houses out of large appliance boxes, for instance. *Snowy Day* (Ezra Jack Keats) can precede a snowflake-making craft. Websites for teachers or parents who homeschool can be great resources.

If/Then

"If/Then" is a great game to play around the dinner table with a large multi-generational group. Hand everyone a slip of paper on which to write a phrase beginning with "if," such as "If Dad wore something besides plaid shirts …" or "If Grandma liked watching football on TV…." When everyone is done, instruct them all to fold their papers and put them in the middle of the table. Mix the papers up, and let everyone pick a phrase to finish. The answers should begin with "then," as in "…then people would not mistake him for a lumberjack" or "…then Grandpa wouldn't have to sneak over to our house to watch."

Now it's time to read the statements out loud. But rather than read them as written, the first person reads the "if" statement from her paper followed by the person to her right who reads the "then" statement from *his* paper; the two disconnected phrases will sound very funny when read as one sentence! Continue around the table until all if/then statements have been read!

Color Me Happy

Coloring isn't just for kids anymore! A variety of coloring books for adults have come onto the market in recent years (and have hit best-seller lists!), marking a shift in the intended audience for this relaxing pastime. Some coloring books for adults have themes (architecture, anatomy, the Bible…) and others are simply page after page of intricate patterns and designs. Seen as both a creative and calming hobby that harkens back to a simpler time, coloring is something that every member of the family can enjoy. In addition, no artistic talent is required to create beautiful pieces of artwork: No one needs to learn a new skill set for this creative outlet! Bring a little zen (and nostalgia) to your Family Fun Nights with coloring books!

Clear the kitchen or dining room table and supply everyone with a variety of crayons, colored pencils, and fine-tipped markers. Take turns choosing background music. Or just chat as you color – one of the blessings of this activity is that it doesn't require a great deal of concentration. It can be done in combination with other things.

When your artwork is complete, you can hang it on the refrigerator or on the walls. Many of the pieces truly are worthy of being displayed and each one is unique.

Adult (and children's) coloring books are available online, and at bookstores and many department stores. Visit our website for a list of some of our favorite coloring books and for a link to free coloring pages that can be downloaded.

Family Learning

Learning something new is even better in the context of a Family Fun Night. In the past, adults may have done all the teaching and children all the learning, but rapid changes in technology mean that kids have the upper hand when it comes to all sorts of things: how to find a show on Netflix, how to post on Instagram, how to update a cell phone, and so much more. Let's face it: We need our kids to help us out at least as much as they need us!

Devote an evening to teaching other family members a special skill. For the first half of the night, the older folks can teach the younger ones; switch roles for the second half. Here are some ideas to inspire you...

Parents and grandparents can teach children how to....

- Knit or crochet
- Make a perfect apple pie
- Whistle with a blade of grass
- Make a daisy chain
- Tie fishing flies
- Make a French braid
- Play jacks
- Make a newspaper hat
- Set up a model train
- Identify birds or bird calls
- Play old-fashioned games like Red Light, Green Light or Kick the Can

Children can teach parents and grandparents how to...

- Play the latest video game
- Open a Facebook or Twitter account
- Use cool phone apps (or just have fun with your phone!)
- Do yoga poses
- Meditate
- Speak another language
- Impress a crowd with yo-yo tricks
- Use texting slang appropriately
- Make a photo book on the computer

A Family Collection

Starting a family collection can be a wonderful multi-generational project. Collecting has a rich history: In the 1700s and 1800s, wealthy folks traveled far and wide collecting items for fossil, shell, animal, art, and book collections. Upon their return, these items were displayed in special rooms called cabinets of curiosities; eventually these collectors founded some of the first museums.

The process of searching for, acquiring, organizing, and displaying your treasures can occupy many family evenings. Whether you spend time looking online to determine the value of your finds, planning or making a trip to find more items for your collection, or identifying and labeling what you've already found, you will find that family collecting is a lot of fun for everyone. You may even want to join a club or association based on your area of interest, go to a swap meet to make a few strategic trades, or visit a museum to see how various collections are displayed.

Children tend to become interested in collecting things at about 5 years old, starting with items like acorns with their caps on, bottle caps, or buttons, and by 6 or 7 can become immersed in looking for items to add and arranging their treasures in a variety of ways. It's not

WHAT TO COLLECT

The best items for family collecting are hardy enough to withstand a lot of handling, are not extremely valuable, and are inherently interesting to everyone. Here's a list of some things that might be fun to collect as a family:

- snow globes
- coins
- marbles
- chess sets
- Christmas ornaments
- masks
- comic books
- hats
- baseball cards
- action figures

- key chains
- autographs
- bottle caps
- sea shells or sea glass
- magnets
- recipes
- postcards
- PEZ dispensers
- salt and pepper shakers

- family-specific theme (elephants, owls, vintage keys, etc)
- Legos or Playmobil sets
- political pins
- children's books
- knock knock jokes
- teddy bears
- lunch boxes
- old toys

only fun, but great for math and reading skills. Kids learn how to classify and organize their finds, as well as how to decide what to add to a collection and why. Collecting can enhance social skills, too, if your little collectors like to trade or show off their possessions. So although collecting may appeal to children who are on the quiet, contemplative side, they often become more animated when they find other like-minded collectors who share their interests.

Easy Family Crafts

How about hosting a craft night for family members? Just spread newspaper on the kitchen or dining table and select a few projects to tackle (or let each person bring his or her own). Here are some ideas for projects that are simple and involve not much more than a few pieces of paper...

A paper helicopter: Most kids know how to make paper airplanes, but how about a paper helicopter? With just paper, scissors, and a paper clip, you can make a spinning glider that twirls to the ground much like a maple seed does. Children will get a kick out of coloring them and everyone will enjoy watching them dropped from upstairs to the floor below. Head to our website for a link that offers detailed instructions and a template you can download.

TIP

Check out craft or home improvement stores like Home Depot or Michaels for free workshops or demonstrations the whole family will enjoy! Learn to make a birdhouse or picture frame or even a race car with your children or grandchildren!

MY STORY

"Since I was little, my family would have Ballroom Dance nights. We would push aside the dining room table and waltz or swing our way around the room. Once my parents had taught us all the moves they knew, we started pulling up YouTube videos showing more complex moves. It's a wonderful way to spend an evening, and now that I'm at college I drag my friends over for dance nights!"

A paper doll chain: Making the chain is fun, but decorating each character in the chain is even better. Fold a piece of paper like an accordion and then cut out a figure in such a way as to create a row of people holding hands. You can tape several chains together to make a longer chain, or use larger sheets of paper for a different effect. Have each member of the family color or decorate one "doll" to represent him or herself!

A paper pop-up book: Does your gang have a favorite family story? Capture it forever in a pop-up book that you make together! Considering how easy they are to make, pop-up books are quite impressive! (If a book sounds too ambitious, make pop-up cards to send to family and friends!) Our website offers several links to sites that provide directions for making your own book.

TIP

Ever heard of Postcrossing? It's the perfect multi-generational activity, and results in your family receiving postcards via the US mail from all over the world! Check out the link on FamilyFun-Night.org that will let you register and begin sending and receiving postcards. This isn't about creating relationships, just about the fun of discovering interesting postcards in your mailbox regularly!

Family Re-decorating Night

Interested in engaging teens and tweens in multi-generational family fun? Everyone dreams about redecorating or redesigning his or her living space, whether you're a middle schooler who wants to add a gaming or reading nook to his room or a grandparent who wants to turn a closet into a sewing corner.

Take an evening to explore the design and decorating possibilities by borrowing books and magazines from the library and perusing on-line decorating sites. A binder with clear pages will allow each person to create a scrapbook of inspirational photos that have been cut or printed out. Some ideas may just be pipe dreams (the spiral staircase with a slide alongside it, for instance), but other concepts will involve projects that you can plan to tackle together, whether it's re-wiring an old lamp and decorating the lampshade, painting a mural on the wall, or sewing pillows or curtains to change a room's theme or color scheme. No matter what the end result, it's fun to dream together!

MY STORY

"I like to show my grandkids how I made parachuting soldiers when I was little. We used a handkerchief tied to a plastic soldier, but my grandsons use 10-inch square pieces of plastic cut from trash bags and little Lego men. We tie pieces of string from each of the four corners to the figure, then we toss it up in the air and watch it float down."

—Frank, grandfather of six

CHAPTER TEN

OUTDOOR FAMILY FUN NIGHT

Family fun nights aren't limited to indoor activities: All sorts of adventures await those eager to head outside, no matter what the season and no matter where you live.

Make like Magellan and explore!

Stop by the library (or go online) and research an interesting local destination—a cave, an old Native American campsite, the site of an historic fort or a crumbling foundation marking a long-ago settlement—and get a map and directions so that you can find your way there. Hike to the spot you've chosen and take time to explore the area, looking for signs—arrowheads, old bottles, pots and pans—of the people who may have lived there centuries ago.

A metal detector may be the best way to find indications of the area's previous inhabitants: Look for the spot where they threw out their trash and then see

TIDBIT

Some experts estimate that there are millions of arrowheads still undiscovered in North America. Each hunter made many spear and arrowheads every year and they were often left behind either by accident (an arrow that missed its target) or intentionally, hidden in places these hunters planned to return to, and then never did.

HIKING NECESSITIES TO WEAR OR TO PACK IN YOUR BACKPACK:

- Hiking boots or other appropriate footwear for every hiker
- Map and compass
- Water and snacks
- Sunscreen and sunglasses
- Flashlight or headlamp

- Extra clothing, including rain gear
- Fire starter
- Whistle
- First Aid Kit
- Knife

what the metal detector can uncover! You may find old tin cans, barrel hoops, or pieces of farm equipment. The adage "one man's trash is another man's treasure" has never been as true as it is when looking through centuries old dump sites!

Disc Golf

Disc golf is becoming more popular every year; there are now hundreds of disc golf courses across the US. Rather than using a set of golf clubs and a ball, disc golf uses a flying disc (the most common brand being a Frisbee). Players move around a course of 9 or 18 holes throwing a disc from a tee area toward a target.

If you have a formal course near you, head over and try it out. If not, you can create a makeshift course at a public park or schoolyard. Identify targets (a trash can, a lamppost, or park bench—ideally, a target is about 4 feet high) and establish a tee area that is from 200 to 500 feet from the target. Decide how many throws it should take to reach the target from the tee based on obstacles and distance: That becomes par for that "hole." (Par should range from 3 to 5.) Out-of-bounds areas can be determined by natural landmarks, such as a path or river. A player loses a point if his disc lands out-of-bounds, and he continues play from the point where the disc went out. If your playing area is small, just use one target (like a hula hoop), and establish a number of tees around it, with rules as to how the disc must travel (i.e. to the right of the big pine tree and left of the concession stand). Disc golf is scored similarly to golf, with points deducted if a player reaches the target under par, and points added if he is over par, each player aiming for the lowest score possible.

Walking Audio Tour

Do you live in or near a big city? Take a self-guided walk around an interesting neighborhood with an audio guide leading the way! Download an audio walking tour to everyone's portable device and explore on your own timetable. Plug in your earphones and hit start at the same time. Whether it's "Haunted New York," or "meTour - New Orleans Walking Tour," you'll learn... you'll learn all sorts of fascinating things as you all listen and stroll together. Look online for audio tours of places near you!

If you'd prefer to go "old school," or you live in a town with no available audio tour, research an interesting part of town on your own and then map out a walking route that includes the best places to visit. You may want to start at the gravestone of a famous local resident, walk to a mural with an intriguing backstory, and then head to an inn where a U.S. president has stayed. Your local historical society is a great place to go for information.

Go fly a kite!

Supply each member of the family with a kite, head to an open area like a beach or park, and try these fun kite games—then make up your own!

- Have a contest to see whose kite can fly the highest in one minute.

- Follow the leader: One kite leads the way, and the others try to follow its path.

- Have a relay race! Divide your family into two teams, each with a kite. One at a time, members of each team must make the kite do a figure eight in the air, then pass the handle to the next person. The team to finish first wins!

- Compete with the other kite flyers to see whose will be the last kite flying. No interfering with the other contestants!

Broom Hockey

Even folks who've never played ice or field hockey can master broom hockey easily! Head to a safe, empty, paved area. With sidewalk chalk, draw a large rectangular court with goals at opposite ends (or use cones or other markers). In the center of the playing area, draw a face-off circle. (You can use the chalk to keep score on the side of the play area.) Divide your family into two teams (or play with another family!) with a goalie, offensive player and defensive player on each team, and give every player a broom.

To begin play, the offensive players from each team face each other in the circle and, at a signal, begin to sweep at the ball between them. Players sweep the ball to others on their team in an attempt to score by getting the ball into the opponent's goal area. As with regular hockey, hands and feet cannot be used to move the ball.

Tweak your Hide-and-Seek

Hide-and-seek is fun to play the old-fashioned way, but there are variations that can make it even more interesting! Try either one of these:

Sardines: One person is chosen to hide as the others cover their eyes and count to 25. As each person finds the initial hider, she joins him, so that more and more people are crowding into one hiding spot. The one who spotted the hider first is the one who hides in the next round.

Kick the Can: One person is named It. It places an empty can, water bottle, or whatever is handy in a central location and counts to 25 (eyes covered) while the others hide. When It finds someone hiding, that person must return to the location marked by the can. Any player who hasn't been found can sneak over and kick the can, allowing everyone to hide again (including anyone who has been caught). All players are safe until It sets the can back up. The game ends when everyone has been found; the first person to have been caught becomes It in the next round.

Not Your Parents' Tag...

Tag is more fun when it's played with some different rules! Give one of these variations a try!

Chain tag: The player who is It starts running after the others and when she tags someone, that person must hold hands with her. Together, they try to catch someone else. When they do, that person must join hands with them. This leaves just the two "outer" free hands in the line for tagging. When everyone has been tagged, the first player to have been caught becomes the next It.

Shadow tag: Rather than tagging another player out, It must step on the person's shadow; then she becomes It.

Ball tag: It throws a playground ball at the others; they are out when the ball hits them.

Water pistol tag: It shoots at the other players with a water pistol; anyone who gets hit by the stream of water is out.

Monkey-in-the-middle tag: It stands in the middle of a circle as a ball is tossed from one player to another. It tries to tag the player who is holding the ball.

MY STORY

"We like to head out for a family walk in search of something that represents the season: the most beautiful leaf in fall, a heart-shaped stone in summer, the biggest animal track in the spring mud or winter snow. We try not to have a plan, but to wander, letting ourselves be led by whatever interesting things we find."

—*Franny, mother of two*

PARK IT

Leave it loose! Head to a nearby park and bring along items guaranteed to generate fun:

- Flying disc, like a flexible, glow-in-the-dark Frisbee
- Large ball or beach ball
- Foxtail softie
- Bottles of bubbles
- Butterfly or fishing net
- Binoculars
- Flashlights for tag

- Containers for holding bugs and other critters for observation
- Water pistols
- Badminton set
- Jump ropes
- Water balloons
- Kites
- Croquet set

Wacky Races

Competitive running races can be traced back to religious festivals that took place hundreds of years BC; the first several Olympic Games featured only one event: a sprint from one end of the stadium to the other. A traditional race, however, can be a bit ho-hum. Try one of these variations...

Waist race: This race works well for groups of six or more...and it's hilarious! Players on each team line up one behind the other, with each one holding onto the waistband of the person in front of him. On "go," each team runs to a designated line at least 50 yards away, with all players hanging on to one another. If someone lets go or falls, the other team wins!

One-minute race: Designate a racecourse that is relatively short and assign one person to be the timer. As the racers line up, they must relinquish their watches and cell phones. On "go," everyone walks or runs the course, with the goal of completing the loop in exactly one minute. The slowest person might win—or the fastest! It depends on who is best able to figure out how long a minute is!

MY STORY

"Our family makes a real adventure out of picking blueberries. We hike to the top of a mountain and pick wild berries for hours. We cut the top off of plastic milk jugs and slid the handle through our belts so we don't drop the berries! When we get home, we make muffins or blueberry pie together."

—Amy, middle school student

Spur-of-the-moment relay race: Find two crooked sticks, each about a foot in length. Divide the group into two teams and establish a start line and a finish line. Players on each team take turns kicking the stick to the finish line and back until everyone on the team has had a turn. The first team to finish wins. (This is an old Native American game.)

Family Fun with Volleyball

Volleyball has a number of variations that make it even more fun for families to play. Decide which one would work best with your group...

Beach ball volleyball: Use a beach ball rather than a standard volleyball. If it's windy, it'll add a chaotic element that can be fun. If it's a calm day and you have littler kids, they'll be more likely to be able to hit a lightweight beach ball.

All-touch volleyball: No one will feel left out in this version: The ball can't be sent back over the net until every person on a side has touched it.

Towel-ly ball: This works well with four people of mixed ages, with two on each side. Partners hold a towel stretched out between them, tossing and catching the ball using only the towel. You can make it more challenging by having two balls going at once.

Water volleyball: In this derivation, players sit in inner tubes to hit the ball back and forth so that kids who aren't strong swimmers can play (with supervision), too.

TIP

To make a volleyball game more cooperative and less competitive, divide the group into two random teams. As soon as a person hits the ball over the net, he scoots under the net to join the other team. Eventually, the teams will be entirely different from the starting teams and no one will have won or lost.

OTHER WAYS TO HAVE OUTDOOR FUN

- Use water pistols to squirt at balloons and keep them up in the air

- Use water pistols to squirt a beach ball into the opponent's end zone: a bit like soccer, without the kicking!

- Play touch football with a water balloon rather than a football

- Wash all the family cars: Productive and fun for the kids!

- Swing a jump rope in a low circle (like a helicopter propeller); each player jumps over it when it swings near him

- Play monkey-in-the-middle with a beach ball, Frisbee, or Foxtail softie

- Play water limbo! Set the nozzle on your garden hose to deliver a straight stream and then keep lowering it until only one (dry) person is left!

TIP

Forget to bring what you need to play games? Get creative! Fill someone's sock with playground or beach sand, tie a knot at the top, and use it instead of a ball or Foxtail softie.

HOW TO SKIP STONES

Skipping stones is all about selection, spin, and speed. Choose stones that are smooth, uniformly thin and flat, and that fit easily into your hand. (Triangular stones work best for choppy waters.) Stand with the shoulder of your non-throwing arm facing the water, feet shoulder-width apart. Stretch your throwing arm backwards and then swing it toward the water, extending your arm and releasing the stone with a quick wrist snap. The stone should spin across the water, with the first skip about five yards away.

Backyard Bonfire

Nothing brings people together outdoors like a bonfire! The warmth of the fire and hypnotic flicker of the flames draw everyone close. And once the troops are gathered round, you can tell ghost stories, watch for fireflies, cook marshmallows for s'mores, sing campfire songs, or do a little star-gazing!

Here are three games you can play around a bonfire:

1. What Good Luck, What Bad Luck: Like the children's book from the 1960s, this game involves taking turns telling a story that involves something good happening, followed by something bad happening, and on and on. For instance, the first player would say, "What good luck! I got to fly in an airplane today!" The next player would say, "What bad luck: The plane had to make an emergency landing!" Then "What good luck: It landed safely – next to a pile of gold!" And on and on!

2. Five Fast Facts: Go around the circle and ask each person to present five facts about his or her day (i.e. "I traded my cookie for an apple at lunch.") After everyone has gone, each person, in turn, has to recite one fact that is not his or her own with no facts being repeated. This continues, as each person who can't think of a fact is eliminated, until a winner is left.

3. One More Motion: The first player makes any motion (i.e., a clap, finger snaps, whistle); the next person repeats the first player's action and adds one of his or her own. Each player in turn repeats the motions of the previous players and adds one. Anyone who makes a mistake is out; the winner is the one left.

TOP 10 CAMPFIRE SONGS:

- Kumbaya
- Oh Susana!
- Home on the Range
- This Land Is Your Land
- Down in the Valley
- The Circle Game
- On Top of Old Smokey (or Spaghetti)
- Blowin' in the Wind
- Hey-Ho Nobody Home (sung in a round)
- Michael, Row the Boat Ashore

MY STORY

"Wiffle ball games were pretty intense at my house. We had a system with imaginary base runners. Over the garden was a home run, and whenever we hit dad's pitch over, we made sure to do the appropriate victory dance. Great times."

—Ellie, college student

"Drive in" Movie Theater

Turn your front yard into a drive-in movie theater! With just a little planning and a few supplies, you can create a summer drive-in experience in your very own driveway!

Assuming that there are no errant street or vehicle lights that will affect viewing, you can hang a white sheet over the garage door for the perfect movie screen. (Tape it down at the bottom so that a breeze won't interrupt the show!) You will need to connect the video and audio signals from your DVD or Blu-ray player into a projector (your kids will probably be able to figure this out more quickly than you will).

With a bit of help from a parent, little children can turn oversize boxes into "cars" from which to view the show. A few strategic holes and some paper plate wheels can turn a dishwasher box into the perfect vehicle: just add pillows and blankets to make it cozy.

Older kids can line sleeping bags and pillows in the back of a van or SUV with the back left open. Adults can stretch out on lawn chairs. Add bags of popcorn and you're all set for a night out (!) at the movies!

For a list of family-friendly movie ideas, check out the suggestions on our website (www.FamilyFunNight.org)!

MY STORY

"We play a game that is like badminton but is called Doink It. Players have more control because the Doink It™ ball is easier to aim than a birdie. It also travels farther and is less affected by the wind. The paddles are very similar to those used for badminton. We bought our set at a store specializing in games and puzzles."

—*Rawan, mother of three*

CHAPTER ELEVEN

EMBRACING SCREEN TIME FOR FAMILY FUN NIGHT

Screen time often gets a bad rap as far as family time goes, and discussions of how to limit and control it are a hot topic among parents. But in the context of a broad range of activities, watching a movie, playing a video game, or learning a new skill from a YouTube video can be a harmless diversion. Most experts agree that teaching children to set limits on certain activities is better than prohibiting them outright. So whether the no-no is candy or television, show kids how special treats are best when they are intentionally enjoyed in limited quantities.

Video Game Night

When public libraries across the country recently sanctioned video games, many parents grudgingly relented, too. On National Gaming Day, libraries included a nation-wide video game tournament as well as the traditional board game

MY STORY

"My son's favorite part of family video game night is that he teaches everyone else how to play the games. His sisters are learning, but he's definitely the expert. As the youngest child, he rarely has the opportunity to show the rest of us how to do something."

—*Kendra, mother of three*

competitions, an acknowledgement that video games have become an integral part of our society.

Even though many parents are reluctant to join the video game revolution, others are happy to get in on the act, viewing it as an opportunity to bond with pre-teens and teens and to model for them balance and restraint. These parents feel that they can show their kids how quality video games can be enjoyed in moderation. In addition, playing games together allows technology to unite the family rather than isolate kids so that they withdraw.

You may go along with the video game idea half-heartedly, but chances are you'll find at least one or two games that appeal to you. No longer the domain of pre-adolescent boys, video games have become popular family entertainment. Believe it or not, studies have shown that women make up 40 percent of the gaming community! Parents soon find themselves getting excited about the idea of hitting a home run, drag racing, or singing in a rock band—without leaving the family room!

TIP

If you and your kids know what the Entertainment Software Rating Board (ESRB) ratings mean, you'll be able to choose games that you feel are appropriate for your family. The ratings are intended to provide information about the content of games and have two parts: the rating symbol (on the front) that suggests an age range and the content descriptor (on the back) that indicates aspects in a game that may be of concern. The most frequently used ratings are:

- EC (Early Childhood) games are suitable for children three and up. There is nothing that would cause parents concern.

- E (Everyone) games are aimed at children six and older. There may be minimal animated or fantasy violence or mildly inappropriate language.

- E10+ (Everyone 10 and older) titles may include more cartoon, fantasy, or mild violence and mildly offensive language. There may also be limited suggestive themes.

- T (Teen) games are appropriate for those 13 and over. These titles may contain violence, suggestive themes, offensive humor, limited blood, simulated gambling, and limited strong language.

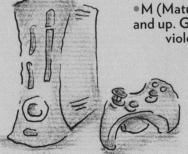

- M (Mature) titles are aimed at those 17 and up. Games rated "M" may include violence, blood and gore, sexual content, and strong language.

Content descriptors include a wide range of elements from alcohol and drug references to nudity.

TIDBIT

Americans spend more than $25 billion a year on video game purchases.

More than 56 percent of households now own at least one video game system.

One big reason that video games have become more popular with families is the greater diversity of games. Games are no longer limited to hurling grenades or jabbing with swords; manufacturers of the top gaming systems offer an incredible variety of themes—from yoga to ghost-busting to drag racing to singing in a rock band. Who doesn't harbor a fantasy of singing or strumming on stage before a legion of faithful fans?

When selecting a game for the family to play, pay close attention to the ratings provided by the Entertainment Software Rating Board. They are extremely helpful when trying to determine the specific content of a game.

Check out our website (www.FamilyFunNight.org) for tips on choosing a game system and for a list of family-friendly game titles categorized according to game system.

YouTube University

Did you know that you can learn to do just about anything by watching You-Tube videos? Want to increase the strength of your wi-fi router, pick a lock, or slice a banana without peeling it? Just head to YouTube: You'll be an expert in no time!

For families looking to spend a fun evening learning a new skill, YouTube is the perfect way to go. You are learning in your own home, for free, at your own pace. An endless variety of videos show, step-by-step, how to fool audiences with magic tricks, use chopsticks, master ballroom dancing, decorate holiday cookies, communicate using sign language, do yoga, make origami animals, create beautiful jewelry, tie-dye clothing, shuffle cards —anything you can imagine. Project the chosen video onto a large screen for easy family viewing. After you've all watched the lesson once, try the activity, pausing the video when necessary. Once you've mastered the skill, try it without referencing the video. The best way to approach YouTube University is to use the videos as springboards for family fun.

> **TIP**
>
> Watching YouTube videos is an especially good way for single parents to master those "gender-bender" tasks: Dad can learn to braid his daughter's hair and Mom can learn how to make a marshmallow shooter with her son.

TIP

To avoid the expense and extra chemicals of microwave popcorn, consider buying a relatively inexpensive air popcorn popper. After the popcorn is made, you can add butter or oil and your own spices like powdered Parmesan and black pepper, curry powder and raisins, soy sauce, coconut flakes, or cinnamon-sugar. (For more popcorn recipes, see Chapter 6.)

Movie Night

There's more to family movie night than just popping in a Blueray from your much-viewed collection, or queuing up a flick recommended by Netflix! Add a family-run snack bar, unique popcorn treats, and a post-film critics' corner, and you'll create a memorable night for the entire gang.

The trick is to select a movie that appeals to everyone, and not succumb to the temptation to choose a film intended only for kids. That's easier to do if your children are teens and are more likely to agree with you as to what makes a good movie. If your kids are younger (and would argue that there's nothing better than a SpongeBob Square Pants cartoon marathon), then check out the movie list on our website (www.Family-FunNight.org). These flicks are guaranteed to appeal to all members of the family. To make it more fun, write down the movie titles on slips of paper, fold them, and put them in a jar for a surprise pick. Or take turns choosing movies from our list, or a list that would be acceptable to everyone in your family.

Get the buzz going early! In the days preceding movie night, promote the film so that your kids are looking forward to it! Hang up a poster (with images downloaded from the Internet) announcing the date, time, and location of your feature presentation. "Pay" the kids in play money throughout the week for good behavior, a kind deed, a chore especially well done, or any positive act. The play money can be used at the snack bar to "buy" popcorn or other munchies or

MY STORY

"When our kids were small and insisted on watching animated movies that my wife and I found hard to take, we would play their movie, take an intermission and put them to bed, and then watch our adult feature, like at a drive-in!"

—*Glenn, father of three*

TIP

The night before, the kids can help you make snack necklaces or bracelets to sell at the snack bar. On a piece of new string or licorice, string Honey Nut Cheerios, Froot Loops, and other "O" shaped cereal. Tie the ends to make edible jewelry that the kids can munch on as they watch the movie!

drinks. Buy a roll of tickets like the ones used in movie theaters (from a party or paper goods store) and hand one out to each child a day or two before as his or her ticket to get into the "theater."

Set up your kitchen counter like a real theater snack bar! Offer granola bars or fun-size candy bars, as well as small baggies full of candy, trail mix, Chex mix, pretzels, or other treats. Many snacks come pre-packaged in single-serving sizes for lunchboxes. You can also "sell" juice boxes, bottled water, or cans of soda for a special treat. Of course, brown paper lunch bags full of popcorn will likely be the most popular item for your little moviegoers. You can also mix popcorn with peanuts, raisins, and M&Ms to add a little variety.

You can use movie review sites to jumpstart a great conversation after the movie ends (as well as to help you decide which movies your family will watch in the future). Print out the reviews ahead of time and have them handy as the final credits roll. Don't feel that your kids are too young to be movie critics: Even a five-year old can discuss and analyze a film. For links to websites that offer a variety of reviews and movie information, go to our website (www.FamilyFunNight.org).

If you have a family of cinephiles, consider keeping a log of the movies you watch, with everyone writing comments about what they liked and didn't like about a given film. Your kids will love to look back a few years to see how they felt about the popular movies of the day.

TIP

You can look up fun facts to share with your family about the movies that you watch together by going online. Our website lists some of the best sites for movie trivia (and also tells you where to go for a list of major movie blunders). Here's a sampling of what you might find:

- Anna Popplewell, the actress who plays the oldest sister, Susan Pevensie, in *The Chronicles of Narnia*, is terrified of mice! As a result, every scene in which Susan interacts with mice had to be shot with her stunt double.

- The original script of *Remember the Titans* was full of profanity, but Disney refused to release the movie until every swear word was removed from the script.

- John Travolta plays a woman in *Hairspray* (he plays the main character's mother), and it took him four hours each day to put on the fat suit and make-up.

- In *Night at the Museum*, there are scenes in which Ben Stiller's character, Larry, interacts with a miniature figure of a cowboy named Jedediah, played by Owen Wilson. During filming, Stiller filmed every scene with Jedediah by talking to a toothpick, and special effects teams added in Wilson later.

- Jennifer Lee, the writer and director of *Frozen*, was the first woman to direct a film that grossed more than $1 billion at the box office.

Finally, don't overlook the special commentary or bonus features section of the movie! (A later release of a film is more likely to have special features.) You'll find a lot of substance there, with "making of" scenes, director's commentary, interviews with the actors, and deleted scenes. A director may comment on why a scene was deleted. Does your family agree with his or her decision? You may learn why an actor decided to take on a certain role, or why an action scene was filmed the way it was. For example, on the two-disc special edition of *Chronicles of Narnia,* a special feature shows viewers how each of the creatures was created through make-up, costumes, and special effects like green screen. Interested in knowing how the Minotaurs or goblins evolved from sketches to final realization? Find "Evolution of an Epic" and click on "Creating Creatures." You'll be amazed!

Be a TV star for Family Fun Night

Believe it or not, you can find inspiration for Family Fun Night by flipping through the television channels! Family-friendly game and reality shows can spark ideas for games your family can play – and record for later viewing! Here are a few ideas to get you started:

"Chopped"

Chopped is a cooking game show in which four chefs compete against one another to win prize money. The twist is that contestants must use a basket of mystery ingredients to create a dish that is judged on taste, presentation, and creativity. After each of three separate rounds (appetizer, entree, and dessert), one contestant is "chopped," leaving just two by the final round.

MY STORY

"We got so excited about filmmaking one year that we decided to make our own movie. We wrote up a script and my husband filmed while the rest of us acted it out. My oldest daughter used a program on her computer to edit it and add music. It turned out great!"

—Maryanne, mother of five

You can replicate this concept with your family in a variety of ways: Allow each family member to take turns choosing five ingredients from the refrigerator or pantry, or give each person $10 at the grocery store to buy ingredients—and then insist that they swap their purchases with someone else in the family for an unexpected twist, or pair up (to help the younger ones) and have each team choose ingredients blindly from a box. No matter how the cooks get their ingredients, each one must turn his or hers into a scrumptious dish that will be judged by the others!

"Wipeout"

Wipeout was a game show in which contestants tried to successfully complete a gigantic, treacherous obstacle course. It had a can't-look-away quality to it and in 2010, won Entertainment Weekly's Guilty Pleasure Reality Showdown award.

You can set up a tamer version of the Wipeout course in your own backyard! See who can complete it the fastest, with the fewest errors. You probably already have everything you need to create an interesting and formidable course. Consider what you could do with a giant exercise ball, a homemade see saw, a hula hoop, old tires, cardboard boxes, ropes, a picnic table, a ladder, foam pool "noodles," traffic cones, tree stumps, and hay bales. Set a stop watch, line up the contestants, and then GO!

"Are You Smarter Than a Fifth Grader?"

This quiz show features a contestant who tries to answer questions based on material taken from elementary school textbooks. Two questions are chosen from every grade level (first to fifth) for a total of ten, with a bonus question at the end. The contestant may have help from a "classmate" (one of the young members of the show's cast). Anyone who cannot answer all of the questions must announce that he or she is "not smarter than a fifth grader."

Families can create a number of variations on this theme. Children can write down questions for their parents to try to answer based on what they have learned recently in school, or a parent can go online to find ten sample questions to mimic the show's format, such as:

- What is the fastest bird on foot?

- What is the capital of Colorado?

- How many sides does a heptagon have?

- What is the lowest prime number?

- Who was the first person to stand on the moon?

- On what continent were most Inca civilizations?

- How old must someone be to serve as President of the United States?

- Are a person's right and left lungs the same size?

- The adult human body has how many bones?

- What is 20% of 240?

Offer prizes—or consequences—that really matter, such as swapping chores or selecting the radio station in the car for a whole week. No matter what the format, the losers must state that they are, in fact, "not smarter than a fifth grader!"

CHAPTER TWELVE

IDEAS FOR LAST-MINUTE FAMILY FUN NIGHTS

Don't forgo Family Fun Night just because everyone is busy! Keep the tradition going with a quickie version of the event. Choose games that need no advance planning and can be played during dinner: You'll still have fun and no one will have to miss soccer practice or play rehearsal. Make a simple meal, grab take-out, or have food delivered. (Think beyond pizza and Chinese: Many traditional restaurants offer menu items to take out.)

Here are 26 terrific ideas for games your family can play without leaving the dinner table!

"What's under the napkin?"

MY STORY

"We like to play a game called 'Roses and Thorns.' We go around the table and take turns talking about the best and worst things that have happened to us in the past week. Even on those weeks when I think I'm aware of everything's that happened, I'm always surprised by someone's story!"

—*Christine, mother of three*

1. Endless Order

One person begins by saying, "For dinner, I want a hot dog." The person next to her says, "For dinner, I want a hot dog and some green beans." The next person says, "For dinner, I want a hot dog, some green beans, and tater tots." Each person continues to repeat the list and add one item until someone gets it wrong and the game starts over.

2. Name That Tune!

Players take turns humming the tune to a popular song as the others try to guess the song's name. Guess correctly, and you get to choose the next hummer!

3. Telephone, with a Twist

Send two whispered messages in opposite directions around the table. The messages will criss-cross as they travel, making it doubly hard to remember the original sentences!

4. Word of Mouth

Mouth a sentence to the person across from you; she has to guess what you said. No repeating the sentence!

5. Trivia Contest

Take turns posing questions to the group from Trivial Pursuit cards (disregard the game board and pie pieces). The youngest should have a chance to guess first.

FOUR BOOKS THAT WILL TURN DINNERTIME INTO GAME TIME

Zobmondo!! The outrageous book of bizarre choices, by Randy Horn. Would you rather...have regular encounters with aliens and not have proof OR have your best friend be invisible? Hundreds of "would-you-rather" questions will keep you dinner discussion interesting!

Can You Beat Ken? edited by Peter Crowell. This trivia book allows you to match wits with Ken Jennings, the all-time Jeopardy champ! It touts itself as "a book you can play!"

The Kids' Book of Questions by Gregory Stock, Ph.D. The hundreds of questions posed in this book will provoke many interesting conversations!

National Geographic Kids Quiz Whiz: 1,000 Super Fun, Mind-bending, Totally Awesome Trivia Questions by National Geographic Kids. See if you can stump the kids—or if they can stump you!

6. Storyteller

Each person takes a turn grouping ten objects on the table and then choosing someone to make up a story that includes all ten objects. When the tale is over, the storyteller can put ten different objects on the table and choose someone else.

7. Family Trivia

Each person in turn asks the group a question about him or herself, such as: "What game do I always play at recess?" "What is the first thing I do when I get to school/work?" "If I could do anything, what would I like to do on vacation?" "What was my happiest moment ever?" "What was my nickname when I was in first grade?" Think you know everything there is to know about your kids or your partner? Guess again!

8. What's the Spoon Tapping?

Take turns hitting nearby items with your spoon while the others listen with their eyes closed and then offer guesses.

9. What's the Category?

Think of a category (things that are funny, things that you would find in Dad's closet...) and start listing items that would fall under the category. Who will guess that "car keys," "sunglasses," and "your mind" fall under the category of "things people in this family often lose"?

10. Big Cheese

While one person closes his eyes, the family selects someone to be the Big Cheese. When the person opens his eyes, the Big Cheese begins an action such as finger snapping, hand clapping, feet stomping, or fork tapping. The others immediately copy what he's doing. When he changes the action, the others follow. The person whose eyes were closed must guess who is playing the part of the Big Cheese. The Big Cheese for one round becomes the guesser for the next. Hint: The players must not watch the Big Cheese too closely or they will give him away!

11. Penny Slide

Take turns sliding pennies across the table, trying to get as close as possible to the target (the sugar bowl) without hitting it.

TIP

Mad Libs (from Price Stern Sloan) are ideal for last-minute Family Fun Nights. These fill-in-the-blank word games cover a wide variety of topics, from dinosaurs to camping. Tear out your favorite Mad Lib and tape it on the refrigerator to remind everyone how much fun you had.

12. Mystery Adverb

While one person covers his ears, the others choose an adverb to describe how they will conduct themselves at the table—slowly, loudly, sadly, seriously... When the person removes his hands from his ears, he has one minute to watch how everyone behaves before he tries to guess the adverb. (Let him offer three guesses before he must give up.)

13. Never-Ending Sentence or Never-Ending Story

One person says the first word of a sentence or the first sentence of a story. The person next to her continues the sentence or the story. The games ends when the sentence gets ridiculously long or the story just gets ridiculous (and it will!).

14. Categories

"My friend Sam likes cookies, but not cake. He likes needles, but not thread. He loves doodling but hates drawing." Another person can chime in at any time: "Does he like bees but not wasps?" The first player would say, "Yes, he does" and the guesser would ask, "Is it because Sam likes things with double vowels?" The answer would be, "Yes!" The category can be as simple as things beginning with "c" or as tricky as "things you would find in a classroom."

15. What's Missing?

Remove something from the table while the others' eyes are closed. Who can guess what was removed?

16. Word Association

This is a silly game that requires little thought or concentration. One person says a word, any word, and the person next to her says the first word that comes to mind. The person next to her reacts to the second word and so on. The spoken words might go something like: car, plane, vacation, beach, bikinis...

17. Three Strikes

Someone begins the game by saying a letter. The next person offers up another letter, and must have a word in mind that begins with these two letters. The third person adds another letter, again with a word in mind. The object of the game is NOT to end the word, but to keep it going. Anyone who ends a word—even if it wasn't the one he had in mind—has a strike. If one player doesn't believe that another has a real word in mind, he can challenge and ask, "What's your word?" If the player does have a word, the challenger has a strike. If he doesn't have a word, he has a strike.

18. Who's Holding the Coin?

One person is designated the guesser. A coin is passed under the table from one person to another (excluding the guesser). At any point, the guesser can say, "Time!" and everyone must put their closed fists on the table. Can the guesser figure out who is holding the coin? If he's wrong, the person holding the coin can keep it. If he's right, he gets the coin and the person who had been holding it becomes the guesser.

19. Would You Rather...?

The classic word game for sleepovers, Would You Rather involves asking players to choose between two equally unappealing scenarios, and then defend the choice. Here are a few dilemmas to get you started:

Would you rather...

...have hiccups forever or be on the verge of a sneeze forever?

...have knives for fingers or for toes?

...have everyone be able to read your mind all the time or wear a clown suit every day for the rest of your life?

...have short arms like a T-Rex or a long neck like a Brontosaurus?

...shout every word you say or silently mouth every word?

20. Toothless Dinner

Take turns naming something that your family has eaten for dinner—without showing your teeth! Each food item can only be mentioned once. If you laugh—or if anyone can see your teeth—you're out!

21. Two Truths and One Lie

Go around the dinner table and take turns talking about your day, but say two things that actually happened and one thing that is a lie. Can the others pick out the lie?

22. Who Am I?

Write down the name of a famous person on a Post-It note. Without showing it to the person on your right, stick the note on his or her forehead. Now the person "wearing" the Post-It note must ask yes or no questions to try to figure out the name on the note. Guessing is harder than you think, so choose someone the player is likely to guess! (Once the guesser reaches 20 questions, you can provide the mystery person's initials as a helpful hint!) Tweak: For younger kids, write the names of animals on the Post-It notes. Players can either answer yes or no questions or make animal sounds to help the one "wearing" the animal's name guess correctly.

TIP

Fill a basket on the dinner table with games for impromptu fun:

- Jump All But One triangle game with golf tees

- Mad Libs

- Trivia books and cards, such as the Fact or Crap cards

- Coffee stirrers to use as pick-up-sticks

- Dice for games like Farkel or Stack

- Rubik's cube

- Magnetic rocks

- Scrabble letters

- Blacksmith or tavern puzzles

- Dominoes

- Deck of playing cards

23. Freeze

Starting with the youngest one at the table, take turns being "It." At a random point during the meal, "It" freezes completely. As soon as the others notice, they immediately freeze too. The last person to notice and freeze, loses.

24. Crazy Talk

Before dinner starts, ask everyone to write down an odd sentence on an index card and place it face down under the plate of the person next to him. Each person then silently reads his sentence and memorizes it. At some point during dinner, everyone must work the assigned sentence into the conversation without anyone noticing. The winner is the one who uses her sentence first without being called out, and the losers are the ones who are caught slipping their sentences into the conversation, as well as the one who uses her sentence last. Here are some sample crazy sentences:

- *I'd like to see if I can eat 20 cucumbers in one day.*
- *I was just thinking about the time that I went to the movies with my imaginary friend Lucille.*
- *I am afraid of fish, even pictures of fish.*
- *When I grow up, I want to be the Abominable Snowman.*
- *I have a pet spider, a Daddy-Long-Legs named Ed.*
- *Sometimes I like to sing the Happy Birthday Song for no reason at all.*
- *If I could only eat one food for the rest of my life, I would pick lima beans.*

25. What's in the Box?

Put something in a shoebox and put it in the middle of the table. In turn, everyone may ask a yes or no question in an attempt to determine what's in the box. (A player must wait for his turn to take a guess. If he guesses incorrectly, he loses his turn and can't ask a question.) The person who guesses correctly chooses the next secret item to put in the box. Tweak: For younger kids, hide something from the table under your napkin while everyone's eyes are closed. Who can guess what it is? (No touching!)

26. Plastic Wrap Ball of Fun

Before play begins, a parent wraps any number of small treats in layers of plastic wrap (with the best one at the very center), creating as large a ball as desired. To start, the first player begins unwrapping the ball quickly, working to uncover a treat, as the player to her right rolls a pair of dice in an attempt to roll doubles, which will end the first player's turn. When her turn ends, the ball and the dice are passed to the right and play continues, with each player keeping the treats she uncovers and each dice thrower trying to roll doubles as quickly as possible to keep other players from getting too many treats! To make the game more challenging, players can wear gloves or the ball can be made of many individual pieces of plastic wrap going in all different directions!

CHAPTER THIRTEEN

IDEAS FOR THRIFTY FAMILY FUN NIGHTS

You don't have to spend a lot of money to have a terrific time with your family. In fact, sometimes the best and most memorable activities are ones that cost next to nothing. The ideas outlined in this chapter may require an investment of your time, but they won't require you to open your wallet. (The change in your pocket should suffice.)

TIDBIT

According to the most recent data from the Bureau of Labor Statistics, the average American family spends about $2,500 each year on entertainment and recreation. Of course, this figure increases with larger families. That's quite a chunk of your family's annual budget!

Here are 12 Family Fun Nights that cost less than $10 each!

1. Family Olympics

Your family can set up an Olympics-style competition that will challenge young and old alike! The key is to come up with a series of events that create a level playing field so that age as well as physical size and strength are not necessarily advantages. Some ideas for "Olympic" events are:

Longest Flight: Everyone has five minutes to make a paper airplane, after which the competitors line up and prepare to throw their creations. The person whose plane flies the greatest distance wins.

First Bubble: Hand everybody a piece of bubble gum and tell them to start chewing. Who will be the first one to make a bubble larger than two inches across?

Hoops: Everyone gets 10 pairs of rolled-up socks and stands the same distance away from an empty wastebasket. Who can make the greatest number of baskets?

Word Search: Each person has three minutes to find the most words within the phrase "Family Fun Night." Kids can make two and three letter words; adults' words must have at least four letters.

Woozy Walk: Spin players around five times and then have them try to walk along a straight line you've laid on the ground with a piece of masking tape. Who can stay on the line?

Thumb Wrestling: Thumb wrestle in pairs with winners playing each other until you have a champion!

2. Personal Pictionary

Make your own Pictionary-type game! In advance, a parent can write or type words on slips of paper, fold each one, and put them all in a jar. When it's time to play, each person can take a turn choosing a word and drawing a picture of it while the others try to guess what she is drawing. If someone guesses correctly, he and the artist each get one point.

3. Science Experiments

You and your kids can conduct fascinating scientific research with objects you have around the house. A number of excellent books and websites can provide detailed information. To get started, try these three experiments:

MY STORY

"One of my favorite childhood memories is when my family had a Rock, Paper, Scissors tournament. We dressed up in costumes and came out like wrestlers. We laughed the whole night and kept the completed bracket sheet on our refrigerator."

—Shelby, college student

Exploding Colors: Pour just enough milk into a pizza pan or baking dish to cover the bottom. Add a few drops of food coloring to the milk in the center of the pan. Squeeze two or three drops of dish detergent on top of the food coloring and watch the fireworks! Read about hydrophobic molecules to find out what happened.

Rocket Launcher: Pour 1/2 cup of water and 1/2 cup of vinegar into a one-quart soda bottle. Put 1 teaspoon of baking soda in the middle of a 4-inch x 4-inch piece of paper towel and twist the ends together to keep the baking soda in place. Once outside, push the paper towel full of baking soda into the bottle and press on a cork top. (You can use a tack to attach streamers to the cork for added effect!) Stand back: The baking soda will react with the vinegar and the cork will shoot into the air! Read about carbon dioxide gas to find out what happened.

Bottled Egg: Find a glass bottle with an opening that is slightly smaller than an egg. Drop a small piece of paper and a lit match into the bottle. Immediately place a hard-boiled egg (with no shell) on top of the bottle, covering the opening. Even though it is larger than the opening, the egg will drop into the bottle! Read about vacuums and high and low air pressure to find out what happened.

4. Puzzle Race

If you think that doing puzzles is too tame, try this twist! Each member of the family chooses a puzzle. (If you don't have enough for everyone, puzzles can be purchased at your local Dollar Store for—you guessed it—one dollar.) Dump all of the puzzle pieces into a pile, mix them up, then... BEGIN! Who can find all the right pieces and finish his or her puzzle first?

5. Spit-It-Out Trivia Contest

You'll laugh your way through this trivia game, win or lose! In advance, make a list of trivia questions and answers (from the Internet, game cards, or books). At game time, divide the family into teams of two: partners will take turns asking and answering the questions. Each team has one minute to get as many right answers as possible. Here's the catch: Place a bowl of Saltines or Ritz crackers in the middle of the table. Every time a teammate answers a question correctly, the player posing the questions must eat a cracker. By the time a player is asking his tenth question, his partner can barely understand what he is saying!

> ### TIP
> Peruse a thrift store for games that can be played whether all the pieces are in the box or not. Trivial Pursuit cards, for instance, can be used without the game board. Collect cards, dice, playing pieces, spinners, and timers to create your own one-of-a-kind game.

6. Make-Your-Own Mad Libs

Mad Libs are funny enough on their own, but when you take the time to create personal stories for your own family, you'll never stop laughing! Study a few Mad Libs to see how they're written, then write your own unique stories and have your family members fill in the blanks!

7. Balloon Football

If your group is looking for a little more action on Family Fun Night, play a gentle version of football. Divide your group into two teams and line up about 30 feet from one another. Each team should position a goalie behind the opposing team who must remain standing on a chair holding a pin throughout the game. Each team tries to hit the balloon toward its own goalie so that the goalie can pop the balloon and score a point for his team. At the same time, the opposing team tries to prevent the point from being scored. The balloon must stay in the air at all times. Note: Have plenty of balloons on hand!

8. Game of Giants

Make your own game board by placing old magazines on the floor in two rows of ten "spaces" (marked by magazines) each. Divide the family into teams and come up with a game token for each team (such as a stuffed animal). Using two sets of trivia cards, one for kids and one for adults, take turns asking and answering questions. A team moves ahead one giant space for each correct answer!

9. Soda Bottle Bowling

Pour a few inches of water into (and then cap) a set of 2-liter soda bottles; set them up like bowling pins. Take turns kicking a soccer ball into the pins to see who can knock down the most.

MY STORY

"We play a tabletop version of shuffleboard that the kids love. I use painter's tape to create a shuffleboard triangle on the dining room table. We use the caps off of milk or water bottles to slide across the table the way you would slide traditional shuffleboard pieces, and we play and score by the same rules. A taste of retirement living in our own kitchen!"

—*Charlie, father of three*

"There once was a monster who loved marshmallows.
As she got into bed, she heard a noise.
INSPECTOR MOUSTACHE CLIMBED OUT OF A HOLE..."

TIP

Ask older relatives what they did for fun when they were young. You'll get some great ideas for thrifty activities!

10. Wacky Story Time

Give everyone a piece of paper and a pen, and instruct them to write the first sentence of a story. When you say "now," each person folds the paper back so that the sentence is hidden, and passes it to the person on his right. Then, each person writes the next sentence of his story and at "now," folds and passes the paper again. Everyone is writing a continuation of his own story, but on a different piece of paper each time. After a pre-established number of passes, everyone reads aloud the story on the paper he is holding, connecting the sentences as naturally as possible.

11. Bend over... and over... and over...

Put a paper grocery bag on the floor in the middle of a room. Take turns coming forward and leaning over to pick up the bag with your teeth. Only your feet can touch the floor and only your mouth can touch the bag—and no props are allowed! After everyone's had a turn, tear off the top inch or two of the paper bag and start the second round. Keep going until you have a winner: The winner is the last one who is able to lean over and pick up the shrinking bag with his or her teeth!

MY STORY

"We like to make gingerbread cookies and decorate them to look like people we know. Then we go around and deliver them!"

—Maria, middle school student

12. Bake Off!

Make cake batter from a mix and divide it among the family members. Each baker can add any ingredients he or she wants—marshmallows, chocolate chips, candy bits, nuts—and then each of the concoctions is put into a muffin tin and baked according to the directions on the package. When the mini cakes are done, each baker can decorate his or hers with frosting and other toppings. Select winners in each category: Presentation, Taste, and Creativity.

CHAPTER FOURTEEN

CARD SHARKS NIGHT

Historians can trace playing cards back to the 10th century, when the Chinese began using paper dominoes the way we use cards today. There are also indications that Chinese gamblers at that time used actual paper money as cards, playing with and for the money. No one knows how and when cards made their way to Europe, although by the mid 15th century, historians note references to playing cards in England. During the reign of Edward IV, cards were allowed to be played only during the 12 days of Christmas!

Fortunately, for us, playing cards is a lawful, year-round pastime. Popular with multiple generations, card games are perfect for Family Fun Night. Games like Seven Card Stud are especially appealing to teens, and they will help entice them to stay home on a Friday night. There are hundreds of terrific family games; just a handful of favorites are described here to get you started, with the easiest games listed first.

TIDBIT

Over the years, there were many different suit symbols used. Before the traditional hearts, spades, clubs, and diamonds were established, symbols like wine pots, books, cups, and a variety of animals appeared on cards.

Spoons

Few card games serve up the kind of excitement that Spoons does!

What you need:
  Standard deck of cards
  Spoons (one fewer than the number of players)
  3 or more players

Goal:
  To collect four cards of one kind and to avoid being the one without
  a spoon

How to play:

To begin, place the spoons (one fewer than the number of players) in the center of the table within reach of all players. Four cards of one rank are required for each player, meaning that if you have just four players, you'll use just the Aces, Kings, Queens, and Jacks. Once the dealer has chosen the cards to be used, she shuffles them and deals out four to each player.

When the dealer says, "Pass," players simultaneously discard one card face down to their left and pick up the card that the player on their right has discarded. Play continues this way, as quickly as possible, until someone collects four of a kind. When this happens, he takes a spoon: He can grab it or quietly sneak it. As soon as other players notice, they must all grab for spoons. The player left without a spoon loses the round and is given the letter "S," the first letter in "SPOONS." When a player has amassed enough letters to spell out the word, she's out.

The player left at the end is the winner.

Variation: *If grabbing for spoons is too aggressive, a player who finds he has four of a kind can place his finger on his nose; the last one to copy his action is out.*

MY STORY

"We play cards for pennies, rocks, jellybeans—even seashells (when we were on vacation at the beach)! We have a jar in the kitchen where we toss our pennies so that we have enough to play with on our family card nights."

—*Steve, father of four*

Slapjack

Anyone who can recognize the Jack can play this fast-paced game.

What you need:
Standard deck of cards
2 to 4 players

Goal:
To win all the cards in the deck

How to play:
The dealer shuffles and deals the entire deck of cards face down. Players may not look at their cards but should tap them into a neat pile.

Moving quickly, each player in turn takes the top card from his pile and slaps it face up in the center of the table. When the card is a Jack, every player tries to slap his hand on top of it. The first to put his hand on the Jack wins the entire pile of cards. The winning player shuffles the new cards into his existing pile. Play continues.

If anyone mistakenly slaps a card that is not a Jack, he must give the top card from his pile to the player whose card he slapped.

Players who run out of cards are out; the game continues until someone wins all of the cards.

TIP

Many websites feature video series to teach viewers a variety of ways to shuffle cards. Find links at www.Family-FunNight.org!

TIDBIT

Packs of playing cards in Italy, Spain, Germany, and Switzerland do not have Queens.

Match Up

This simple game is great for kids who are new to cards because they must learn to recognize suits.

What you need:
  Standard deck of cards (Ace is high)
  2 or more players

Goal:
  To be the first player to get rid of all of your cards

How to play:

The dealer shuffles and deals seven cards to each player; the rest are placed facedown in the middle of the table as stock cards. Players may look at the cards they were dealt.

The player to the dealer's right places any card from his hand face up on the table. In turn, players must place a card on the previous one that matches its suit or number. For example, if a player puts down a three of clubs, the next player must play either a three or any clubs. If he doesn't have an appropriate card, he must draw from the stockpile until he finds a suitable card. If he takes every card in the pile and still doesn't get one that is the right number or suit, he passes and the next player continues. When every player has played all his cards or passed, the one who played the last card must play a new card to start a new round.

The first player to put down all of his cards wins.

TIDBIT

The Joker was added to the familiar 52-card deck sometime in the 1860s because players felt that an extra trump card was needed.

Liar, Liar

You may recognize this as a family-friendly version of the game "B.S."

What you need:
  Standard deck of cards (Ace is low)
  2 to 5 players

TIP

Five fun family games you already know how to play

• Go Fish

• War

• Old Maid

• Concentration

• Crazy Eights

OLD MAID

Goal:
To be the first player to get rid of all of your cards

How to play:
The dealer shuffles and deals the entire deck. Players may look at and organize their cards.

One player (usually the one to the left of the dealer) begins by placing between one and four Aces face down in the center of the table, saying aloud the number of cards he is putting down, such as, "Three Aces." The player to his left must place from one to four twos face down, again, announcing it out loud, and the next player, threes, and so on. The cards must be in sequence.

Here's the catch: Because the cards are being placed *face down*, players don't have to play the cards they are reporting. If a player doesn't have the card that is supposed to be played, for example a six, she can bluff by putting down a three and calling out, "One six."

After each turn, anyone who suspects that the last player was bluffing can say, "Liar, Liar!" and turn over the card in question. If the player was bluffing (for example, he called out, "Two threes!" but instead played two Kings), he must add the entire pile of cards to his hand. If he did not lie, however, and the cards he put down were the ones he announced, then the player who called his bluff by shouting "Liar, Liar!" must add the entire pile to her hand!

The first player to run out of cards wins.

President

You can simplify this game by removing the hierarchy and following the basic rules, playing as many rounds as time permits.

What you need:
  Standard deck of cards (Ace is high)
  3 or more players

Goal:
  To be the first player to get rid of all of your cards

How to play:
The dealer shuffles and deals the entire deck to the players. (It doesn't matter if the hands aren't perfectly even.) Players may look at the cards in their hands.

The player to the left of the dealer places a card in the middle of the table. Play continues to the left, with each player putting down a card that is equal or higher in rank to the previous one. If the first player plays doubles or triples (meaning two or three cards of the same rank), all subsequent players must play doubles or triples. Players cannot play doubles or triples unless the first player started the round with doubles or triples.

If a player cannot put down a card that is equal to or higher than the previous card, he must pass. Players can also choose to pass if they do not want to play their cards at that time. If every player passes, then the pile is cleared and the person who played the last card starts the next round with any card or cards (typically a lower card, because they're more difficult to get rid of).

Game play continues until one player runs out of cards. He wins the round and is declared the President (see "hierarchy").

Special rules:

Skipping: If someone plays the same card on top of what was just played (for example, if a player plays an Ace and the next player also puts down an Ace), the next player skips his turn.

Socials: If a player plays one, two, or three cards of a certain rank and another player has the remaining one, two, or three cards of that rank in her hand, she can play all of them immediately (even if it isn't her turn) by shouting "Social" before another player has a chance to make a play. The player who uses a "Social" may then put down any card she desires to begin the round again.

Twos: Twos can be used to clear the pile. The player who uses the two can then start the round with any card or cards in her hand.

Hierarchy: The winner of each round is declared the President and the loser of each round is declared an Average Joe. When the next hand is dealt, the Average Joe must give his best card to the President, and the President gives her worst card to the Average Joe. The President then starts the new round. For added fun, your family could allow the President of each round to sit in a special chair (or offer up another fun perk), because there will likely be a different President after each round.

Black Lady Hearts

This classic card game can also be fun to play in teams! In a group of 4 or 6, the player sitting across from you becomes your team member, and the two of you combine your scores at the end of each round.

What you need:
    Standard deck of cards (Ace is high)
    Pencil and paper to keep score
    2 to 6 players (4 is ideal)

Goal:
To avoid the Queen of Spades and all heart cards, or to "shoot to the moon" by taking every heart card *and* the Queen of Spades

How to play:
The dealer shuffles and then deals the entire deck evenly among all players. If it's not possible for players to end up with exactly the same number of cards, remove several of the lowest cards from the deck. Choose one player to keep score.

At the start of each round (the rounds are called "tricks" and consist of each player, in turn, playing one card), players look at their cards and pass three cards of their choosing to the player on the left. (Players generally give away the highest cards in their decks). The player to the left of the dealer begins by playing any card in his deck (except for hearts) face up in the center of the table. In succession, each player must play a card of the same suit. If a player does not have a card of the same suit, she can play any card that she'd like to play, even a heart. Once a heart is played on a different suit (meaning that a suit other than a heart started the trick), players can then begin tricks with hearts. *If players find this rule confusing, it can be disregarded and players can start tricks with hearts as they choose.*

After each person has played one card, the player who played the highest card in the suit that led wins the trick. Note that winning the trick is not always a good thing (see scoring below for details); players want to avoid winning tricks containing heart cards and the Queen of Spades. The player who won the trick starts the next trick by playing any card in his deck. The cards that he won in the previous trick are not added to his hand but placed aside for scoring at the end of the round.

Game play continues until all players are out of cards, ending the first round. Game play continues with subsequent rounds in this manner until one player reaches a previously determined score (50, 75, or 100 points). The player with the lowest score at that point wins, and the highest score loses.

Scoring:

1 point for each heart card won in a trick

13 points if a player wins the Queen of Spades

Shooting the moon: If a player wins all 13 hearts and the Queen of Spades, 26 points are deducted from his score, and 26 points are added to the scores of every other player!

Extra scoring options:

Deduct 10 points for the Jack of Diamonds

Alternate scoring:

Ace of Hearts is 14 points, King of Hearts is 13 points, Queen of Hearts is 12 points, Jack of Hearts is 11 points, ten of hearts is 10 points, nine of hearts is 9 points, and so on. Queen of Spades is 50 points and Jack of Diamonds is *negative* 40 points. Games continue to 250, 275, or 300 points. "Shooting the Moon" scoring changes, too, with 100 points deducted from the player's score, and 100 points added to the scores of every other player!

BUILDING A
HOUSE OF CARDS

Bryan Berg, who holds the Guinness World Record for building the largest house of cards, travels all over the world showing off his special talent. He built a 14-foot tall house in the shape of Cinderella's Castle using 3,000 decks of cards, and he spent 20 days in Hong Kong just before the Beijing Olympics building the Athlete Village in cards. He used 50,000 cards to build a replica of Gotham City in Antwerp to celebrate *Batman: The Dark Knight*.

Building a house of cards is best suited for family members with a great deal of patience, an artistic vision, and most importantly, a steady hand. Here's a tip from the experts: Old, worn-out cards are better for building than newer cards, which tend to be slick. And, unlike Bryan, you'll probably want to start out using just one deck!

"Fun Money" Card Games

Betting card games are great for pre-teens and teens, who always have to assess the "cool" factor before committing to a family activity.

TIP

Everyone has a particular betting pattern. If you can figure out what it is, you have a much better chance of winning! Does the player on your left get talkative when he has a good hand? Does the one across the table always raise when he has a great hand? People tend to be very consistent, so pay close attention to patterns and use them to your advantage!

Given this tip, make sure that none of the other players can recognize your betting pattern! Change it up a bit so that you remain a bit of a mystery.

MY STORY

"We use chocolate coins for betting when we play cards and the kids couldn't be happier about it. I mean, candy and money all in one? C'mon!"

—Leslie, mother of two

Betting terms:

Call: Place a bid that equals the previous bid.

Raise: Place a bid that equals the previous bid plus as many additional tokens as the player is willing to risk. (Subsequent bidders must then meet this raised bid.)

Fold: Drop out. The player gives up and automatically loses the round.

In a standard betting card game, two or more players are required, a standard deck of cards is used (Ace is high), and tokens such as coins or Skittles are needed. The goal of any betting card game is to get the best hand and win the pot (or to bluff and trick all of the other players into folding in order to win the pot).

Scoring

(the following are ranked highest to lowest):

Royal Straight Flush: Ace-King-Queen-Jack-10

Straight Flush: Five cards in sequence of the same suit

Four of a Kind: Four cards of the same rank

Full House: Three of a kind and one pair (between two or more hands, the highest card in the "three of a kind" wins)

Flush: Five cards of the same suit

Straight: Five cards in sequence, not the same suit

Three of a Kind: Three cards of the same rank

Two Pair: Two matches (two cards of one rank, two cards of another rank)

One Pair: One match (two cards of the same rank)

High Card: Highest-ranked card in the hand

Note: Between two or more hands with the same score (for example, two players have a straight), the player with the highest card wins.

TIP

Don't feel you need to play every hand: Fold more often! Beginning poker players tend to play too many hands, staying in just to be part of the action. A general rule is that if you're staying in more than half of the time, you need to reconsider your starting hand requirements.

Blind Man's Bluff

This silly, basic betting card game is great for younger kids, and it's also a perfect way to introduce your family to more complex betting games because the basics of betting and perfecting your "poker face" are introduced in an entertaining way.

What you need:
Standard deck of cards (Ace is high)
Tokens, such as coins or candy
2 or more players

Goal:
To have the highest card and win the pot

How to play:
The dealer shuffles the deck and deals one card face down to each player. The players are not permitted to look at their cards.
The round begins when each player antes up, placing one token in the center of the play area. (Even if a player plans to fold immediately, he must ante up at the beginning of the round.) Each player holds her card on her forehead with one hand during game play so that players can see each one another's cards, but cannot see their own cards. If a player looks at his own card, he's out automatically.

> **TIP**
>
> When playing Blind Man's Bluff, players can lick their fingers and moisten their foreheads so that the cards will stick to their foreheads, leaving both hands free.

Game play begins with the player to the left of the dealer. He looks around the table to determine his chances of having the highest card at the table. The player then has two options: He can place a bid by adding any number of his tokens to the pot (the center of the game play area), or he can fold. Each subsequent player can either call or raise the bid.

Once all bets are in, players remove the cards from their foreheads and compare. High card takes the pot; a tie splits the pot. The dealer deals a new card to each player from the remaining deck. Game play continues until there are no cards remaining in the deck.

MY STORY

Never played card games that involved betting when I was young, so it was really fun to learn the proper terms for wagering and the correct scoring rules with my kids. As soon as we mastered the language, it was so much easier to learn the games together. We use Monopoly money for wagering and have a blast!

—Sebastian, father of three

Acey Deucey

Acey Deucey is easy to learn and fun to play. You might also know this game (or a slight variation) as In-Between, Between the Sheets, or Yablon.

What you need:
2 Standard decks of cards (Ace is high)
Tokens, such as coins or candy
4 or more players

Goal:
To have the third card dealt fall numerically between the first two.

How to play:

Players are each given a stack of tokens; they ante up. The first player is dealt two cards, face up. That player then decides whether or not he thinks the third card dealt will fall numerically between the first two. Based on his guess, he can raise his bet up to the amount in the pool. If the third card does indeed fall between the other two, he takes his winnings. If it falls outside the two cards or is equal in value to one of them, he must add what he bet to the pot.

If the first two cards dealt are consecutive, they are put back in the deck and two more cards are dealt. If the first two cards are the same, the player bets whether the third card will be higher or lower. If the third card is the same as the first two, the player must add triple his bet to the pot.

Once the first player has finished his turn, cards are dealt to the next player, and then the next. If the pot runs out of tokens, each player must put in one chip from his or her stack.

There are a number of variations to the game; this version is the most basic, so it's the perfect way to learn the rules and get started!

Five Card Draw

The rules for Five Card Draw are easy to follow.

What you need:
    Standard deck of cards (Ace is high)
    Tokens, such as chips or candy
    2 or more players

Goal:
    To get the high hand

How to play:
Players ante up. The dealer deals five cards down to each player. Players look at their own hands.

Bets are placed after the initial deal. After the betting round, each player may exchange up to three cards. (If a player has an Ace, he can trade in the other four cards in his hand.) The dealer deals new cards if needed so that every player always has a total of five. Another round of betting follows. Then it's time for the showdown, where everyone shows his cards and the person with the best hand wins.

The game continues until one player has all the chips and is declared the winner.

Standard variations:
Wild Cards: Add wild cards to play.
High/Low: The highest hand and lowest hand split the pot.
Lowball: Lowest hand wins.
Double Draw: After the first exchange and subsequent betting, there is another round of exchange and betting.

Seven Card Stud

This classic game allows for many rounds of betting, which is especially fun for kids.

What you need:
Standard deck of cards (Ace is high)
Tokens, such as chips or candy
2 or more players

Goal:
To have the highest five-card hand

How to play:
Players ante up. The dealer deals each player two cards face down and one card face up. Players look at the cards that were placed face down.

The player with the lowest card showing puts in a small bet; betting continues to the player's left. When the betting is complete, the dealer gives each player one more card, face up. Another round of betting takes place, this time beginning with the player who has the highest cards showing. (From this point on, the player with the highest cards showing bets first.) After this, a fifth card is dealt face up. Another round of betting follows, and then a sixth card is dealt face up. Again, a round of betting follows. The seventh card is dealt face down to the players who remain. After one final round of betting, everyone shows his hand. The player who can make the best five-card hand (from the seven cards he has), wins. Continue the game until one person has all the chips. She is the winner.

CHAPTER FIFTEEN

IDEAS FOR A FAMILY TALENT SHOW NIGHT

If you're ready for a new kind of Family Fun Night, try spending an evening showing off your talents (or lack of talent)! Depending on the range of ability in your group, you can focus on genuine talents (like playing a musical instrument) or silly skills (like blowing giant bubbles with gum), or combine both for an evening of unique and unforgettable entertainment!

If you are a gifted singer or acrobat, then you need no suggestions for a talent show act. If, however, you're like most of us who can barely hit the notes of the *Happy Birthday Song* and couldn't do a somersault (even downhill), then you'll appreciate this list of 20 ideas for talent show acts that require little or no actual talent.

TIP

Don't overlook legitimate (though often unsung) talents within the family! Can your daughter show off her karate moves or twirl a basketball on the tip of her finger? Can your son do yoyo tricks? Can Dad whistle just about anything? Can Mom make amazing shadow puppets? You may have a talented family and not even realize it!

1. Read poetry aloud.

For serious selections, check out Caroline Kennedy's *A Family of Poems: My Favorite Poetry for Children.* For something sillier, try one of Shel Silverstein's wonderful books of poetry.

2. Sing a duet...with yourself!

Dress and make up your left side as a man and your right side as a woman. Lip-sync a song with both a female and a male part. Turn your profile to one side or the other, depending on which voice is singing.

3. Play the kazoo.

Any song will do.

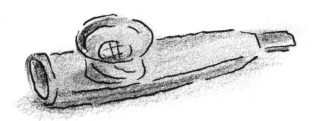

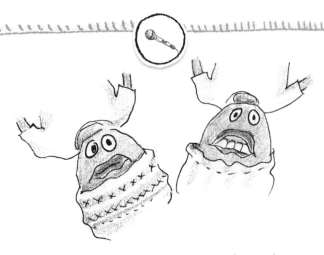

4. Perform a skit with chin faces.

Any act delivered by "chin faces" is sure to be outrageously funny! To prepare, actors lie on their backs (ideally on a large ottoman) so that their heads are upside down. The designated make-up person draws eyes and a nose on each actor's chin and then gently covers the rest of his face so that only the chin and mouth are visible. Then, let the play begin! Actors won't be able to read anything because their eyes will be covered, but they can deliver a pre-rehearsed performance or they can improvise!

5. Juggle scarves.

They float, so even if you've never juggled anything in your life, you'll be able to juggle scarves.

6. Bring Fido into the act.

Show off some tricks you've taught the family pet. (Or come up with your own "tricks" that require the animal to do nothing other than be itself!)

7. Perform a comedy routine.

Get some joke books from the library or go online to find great material.

8. Do impressions...

of each other, the neighbors, the school crossing guard, Uncle Charlie, or even the family pet! Use props and costumes. Make the audience guess who you're imitating, turning your act into a combination of charades and impersonations!

9. Do the Chicken Dance.

(Check out a YouTube version to refresh your memory.)

10. Show off your cup stacking skills!

Often taught in elementary school PE class, cup stacking or speed stacking involves stacking plastic cups in a pyramid and then unstacking them – very quickly! Although the sport uses regulation cups, you can get away with using your own cups for a family talent show.

11. Hop, skip, and jump.

Practice jump rope tricks and then show off the best ones to the family.

12. Play The Question Game with a partner.

No need to rehearse for this performance; it's best as an impromptu act. The simple premise is that the entire conversation must consist of questions. Keep going until someone can't come up with a logical question and then start a different conversation, or pull someone else on "stage" to play.

TIP

Play an instrumental CD in the background when non-musical acts, like yoyo stunts or magic tricks, are "on stage."

13. "Clink out" a song.

Fill glasses with various levels of water and play a song by tapping them with a spoon. Or make the same glasses sing by running a wet index finger around the rim of each glass.

14. Copy a popular camp routine.

One person stands in front of the other with his hands behind his back. The person in the back slips her arms through the sleeves of the one in front so that it appears that her arms are actually his. Then they act out a previously agreed-upon skit. (Acts involving eating and drinking, putting on make-up, and gesturing are particularly funny!)

MY STORY

"We got my daughter a karaoke machine for her birthday and we love to set it up and sing karaoke as a family! We don't care what we sound like, we just have fun!"

—*Juanita, mother of two*

15. Perform a little magic.

Practice a few card and magic tricks and show off your newfound skills to the rest of the family. Watch YouTube videos or visit how-to sites for ideas.

16. Have a shadow play.

Hang a plain sheet in a double doorway or string it across a corner of the room. Place a spotlight or other strong light bulb about 8 feet behind the curtain so that the beam of light is aimed at the sheet. Turn off all other lights in the room. Actors must stand behind and close to the sheet to create the best shadow. Music can accompany the play, a narrator can read lines, or the actors themselves can speak.

17. Make a peanut butter and jelly sandwich...

with instructions from your kids. Have your kids tell you step-by-step how to make the sandwich and do exactly what they say. If someone says, "Put peanut butter on the bread," take the entire jar and set it on top of the loaf of bread!

18. Hoop it up.

Revisit the '60s by showing off some hula-hoop tricks. Pop onto YouTube to check out videos of hula-hooping techniques to try!

19. Do a little improv acting.

Divide the family into two teams and give each a paper bag filled with assorted (random) objects like a banana, a flashlight, a spoon, a sock, and a stapler. Each team has five minutes to discuss what kind of a play they will perform using all of the objects in the bag.

20. Put on a puppet show.

A spring-tension rod suspended in a doorframe can support a curtain that will hide the puppeteers. Little puppeteers can use an appliance box with an opening cut out so that the puppets can peek out. You can create simple puppets with paper bags, socks, or even your fists!

MY STORY

"My kids put on a shadow play for us that involved a patient complaining of a stomach ache while a doctor extracted all sorts of items from the patient's stomach and discussed each one. It was so funny because the items he pulled out included things like a French horn, a spatula, and a dog's leash!"

—*Nina, mother of four*

Should I check off "person with curly orange hair" or "person with polka dot pants"... or BOTH?

CHAPTER SIXTEEN

FAMILY SCAVENGER HUNT NIGHT

If you're looking for a unique way to bond as a family, embark on a family scavenger hunt! Scavenger hunts have been popular with kids and adults for generations. Today's hunts are much more varied than the ones you might remember participating in as a Boy Scout or at a birthday party years ago. From Internet hunts that don't require participants to leave the living room to spooky graveyard adventures, scavenger hunts can take a variety of forms, and they can be tailored to fit any number of themes, occasions, or locations. Hunts foster teamwork and cooperation among siblings and require them to use their creative problem-solving skills.

When you organize your hunt, decide what your goal is, other than family bonding.

Do you want your kids to become familiar with a certain area of town?

Do you want to have an entertaining video of the event to watch later?

Do you want the kids to learn something new?

Determine how participants will prove what they've seen or done (unless the hunt requires collecting specific items). You may ask for signatures, digital photos, or information filled out on a sheet of paper.

Create a list of items to be "scavenged." Decide if different items have different point values and assign those. Is a signature from Mr. Brown, the cranky neighbor no one ever sees, worth more than a signature from Mrs. Jones, who is warm and friendly and will inevitably offer visitors a slice of pie?

Finally, you may want to do a test run of the hunt to make sure that it is practical and feasible. You can tweak the list if some items seem like they will be too hard (or easy) to find.

There are as many different kinds of scavenger hunts as there are people to conceive them. You are limited only by your imagination (and the level of embarrassment your kids are willing to endure!). Listed here are some of the more popular, as well as a few unique, hunts for families.

Mall Hunt

A shopping mall hunt is especially fun if your kids are pre-teens or teens and are old enough to explore the mall on their own. If you live in an area without a mall, a safe, compact downtown area can work just as well. It's best to have a time limit, as kids can get distracted easily in stores. There are several variations on the Mall Hunt theme:

Organize a traditional Mall Hunt, requiring each team to get the items on a list you've created, such as: a penny found face-up, a compliment from a store clerk, a packet of sugar with the name of a restaurant on it, something that costs less than 25 cents, a brochure for a fun activity in the area, a shopping bag that has red letters on it, or an old receipt for another person's purchase.

> ## TIP
> Be sure everyone has a charged cell phone that is turned on so that you can keep track of the group as they explore the mall.

Give each team a list of clues that will lead them to particular stores. In each store, they will need to get certain things, such as the price of a particular item or a credit card application. If you have the time, you can go to the stores ahead of time and ask the store managers to hand your kids the clue that will take them to the next location. (One group should start at one end of the mall while the other group starts at the opposite end. This way the teams are not following each other from store to store.)

Rather than items to find, you can have the teams complete certain tasks like whistling an entire song in the middle of a jewelry store, trying on a tuxedo or a tiara, saluting a store employee, stretching out on a mall bench, asking a fellow shopper a question in a crazy accent, or sampling something in the food court. You should ask each team to record the events on a cell phone so you can share in everyone's experiences later on.

Give each team five dollars. How many *different* items can each team purchase with its money? (No fair buying 500 gumballs!) Set a time limit and a place to meet when the hunt is over.

Neighborhood Hunt

If you know the neighbors well (or want to get to know them better!), send your family on a hunt in the neighborhood. Two groups can go door-to-door collecting items on a list such as a take-out menu, a used dryer sheet, or a dandelion from a neighbor's weedy lawn. You'll want to let the neighbors know ahead of time that your kids will be stopping by as part of a game. Set a time limit to keep the groups moving right along (and let them know that in the event that both teams are able to get everything on their lists, the team returning home first is the winner). Each team should have the same list of items, but it's best to have them ask for different things from different people.

Photo or Video Hunt

Rather than check items off a list, your scavenger hunt teams can take photos of specific things. Each team can head out with a digital camera or cell phone and a list as well as instructions for a meeting time and place. In a mall, for example, you could ask teams to photograph things like a mannequin with short black hair, a person pushing two kids in a stroller, or people holding hands. You can decide whether one or more team members must be included in each photo.

In an interesting twist on the Photo Hunt idea, you take photos ahead of time of landmarks, signs, statues and other items within walking distance of your house or downtown. Then crop the photos so that only a portion shows. Each team is given a printout of all of the photos and is asked to identify every object within a set period of time. You could photograph the last few letters of graffiti on a building, a unique door or door handle, a parking meter that leans to one side, a brightly painted fire hydrant, and other similarly distinctive objects.

MY STORY

"We organize a scavenger hunt during the winter that the kids just love. Ahead of time, we make colored ice cubes: lots of blue and green ones and just a few reds (they are worth the most points). Then we hide them outside and the kids run around and try to find them. They forget that it's 20 degrees out there!"

—*Jeffrey, father of four*

You could also plan a hunt using cell phone recordings. You'll need to make sure that each team has a cell phone capable of recording all of the action, as well as a list of situations each team is required to record. Team members might be asked to film themselves doing certain things (like helping someone to the car with her groceries or holding an elevator for someone who is trying to get on) or capture specific situations involving other people (a little child jumping over puddles). The situations can require teams to perform helpful acts around town or do silly or challenging things. Each segment shouldn't run longer than a minute to make later viewing easy. Just upload everything onto the computer when the hunt is over!

TIP

For even more outrageous fun, you can mandate that a certain object (a favorite stuffed animal, for example) must be included in every photograph!

Information Hunt

Instead of looking for items on a list, teams embarking on an Information Hunt (armed with a list as well as a map) are looking for specific knowledge. Teams might be asked to find the date on the cornerstone of a building, figure out the phone number of the only remaining pay phone in town, find out what it costs to buy a cup of coffee at a certain restaurant, record the date on a particular tombstone, or other data of interest in your town. The team with the most correct answers within a certain time frame wins.

Treasure Hunt

A treasure hunt is a specific type of scavenger hunt in which a series of clues lead to a final "treasure." One clue leads to the next until the end of the hunt. A clue may be in the form of a riddle or may give directions (walk ten paces and turn left, for instance). A treasure hunt requires someone to set out clues ahead of time in places where they won't be disturbed, like underneath a park bench. Teams compete to see which one will be the first to solve the clues and get to the treasure. You can also have family members work together to reach the final destination where the treasure awaits. The "treasure" can be an object like a movie that the family has been wanting to see or a destination like a favorite family restaurant where you'll then have dinner.

MY STORY

"We hide treasure hunt clues in plastic Easter eggs so that the kids will recognize them. We also make sure they are in places where someone else isn't likely to pick them up and take them!"

—*Caryn, mother of three*

TIP

You can combine various elements from different hunts to create a truly unique experience. You might include things to photograph, things to collect, information to uncover, and clues to solve.

Graveyard Hunt

A Graveyard Hunt is perfect for a Family Fun Night that is close to Halloween and can be done in teams or individually, as you'll all be within a confined area. Create a list of a dozen or so items for everyone to find. (This may require you to visit the cemetery ahead of time to make sure that the items you've listed can be located there.) Rather than having players check items off of a list, provide everyone with paper and crayons or pencils so that they can create rubbings of each item they discover.

Your list can include items like a tombstone with a picture of an animal on it, an epitaph that includes the word "love," a tombstone with someone named "John" on it, a tombstone that lists a birth date that matches someone in the family, or a tombstone that is exactly 100 years old. You can award extra points to the team or person who finds the oldest tombstone, the deceased who lived the longest or the shortest life, the deceased with the longest first or last name, or the tombstone with the most names on it.

Sound Hunt

Scavenger hunters can listen for, rather than look for, items on a list, and record them on a cell phone. The kinds of sounds you can include on a list are a bell ringing, a dog barking, a certain advertisement on the radio, or a train whistle. Certain sounds may be worth more points than others, depending on the likelihood that the players will hear them. You may want to define the area where teams are permitted to go and set an end time. Award the win to the team who records the greatest number of sounds from the list.

Around the House Hunt

The classic scavenger hunt involves searching for designated items around the house or in the backyard and returning within a certain amount of time. The simplest hunt to organize, the Around the House Hunt can require participants to find things as simple as a blue toy, or as tricky as something that doesn't belong in the house or something that is missing a part. You can get silly (requiring people to find sporks or light sabers) or practical (a postage stamp or a ten-year-old penny).

TIP

Make sure you monitor the Internet searches of your younger kids so that they don't stumble across any inappropriate content online.

TIP

For a last-minute, home-based scavenger hunt, divide the family into two teams and hand each group a stack of magazines, scissors, and a list of photos or words to hunt for (a man wearing glasses, a red flower, a sad child, a mitten...). The first team to find all of the items on the list wins! You can set a time limit if you wish.

Missing Pieces Hunt

Your family can work as a team to find the missing pieces of a puzzle or object that you've hidden ahead of time. Hiding them in your house or yard is the easiest and most convenient thing to do, although you can take this hunt to a public area if you're sure other people won't disturb the objects. You can use pieces of a jigsaw puzzle or you can connect this hunt to a theme by, for example, taking apart a plastic jointed skeleton and hiding its pieces for Halloween.

People Hunt

Have your family scavenger hunters search for people rather than things! You could include people you know or complete strangers. As proof that they located the people on the list, players could collect autographs or business cards. The list could include someone named Bill, someone who has at least four children, someone who is or used to be a teacher, someone who looks like a celebrity, and so on. A parent will want to accompany each team for safety reasons.

Wiki-Race

A Wikipedia Race (an Internet scavenger hunt) is perfect when the family wants to stay home, or when you want to play with someone remotely, such as family members in college. All that's needed is a computer with Internet access for each player. (And, if appropriate, make sure "Safe Search" is turned on!) These races are often used as a learning tool for students who need to know how to search the Internet. The game is simple: List two items that are seemingly unrelated, such as "a sloth" and "Burger King." Now, see how long it takes to get from the start (in this case, the Wikipedia page for "a sloth") to the finish line (landing on the Wikipedia page for Burger King) by clicking through the internally linked Wikipedia articles only. In other words, you can only move from one article to another by clicking hyperlinked words within Wikipedia! So, for instance, perhaps within the article for "sloth" you click "insects," which takes you to a new page, where you can search for another hyperlinked word that might, tangentially, eventually lead you to Burger King, and so on. The first one to reach Burger King wins! (As an added bonus, this is great practice for kids who need to look things up for homework.)

TIDBIT

Rick Gates, a library science student, created the first Internet Scavenger Hunt in 1992. He wanted to urge people to explore the many resources on the Internet. He distributed questions through a variety of sites and offered a prize to those who completed the hunt.

Alphabet Hunt

After you've agreed on a theme and location for the hunt, each team heads out with a list lettered from A to Z. In the pre-determined time, each team must find one item that begins with each letter. The hunt can take place in your neighborhood, on a playground, in a shopping mall, or in your own house.

Math Hunt

Put your arithmetic skills to good use in this Math Hunt! This is an easy contest to judge: The team that returns home with the correct answer wins! No need for a team to check items off lists, take photos, or offer anything else as proof of its accomplishments!

This will require a little prep work on your part. You'll need to drive around town (or the designated area for the hunt) and develop a list of questions that relate to familiar landmarks and locations. Then you can create a simple math problem to represent each question. When all of the math problems are worked out in order, you'll have a numerical answer. That's all each team needs to bring home at the end of the hunt!

For example:

The number of mailboxes directly outside the post office

TIMES

The number of gas pumps at the convenience store on the corner

PLUS

The number of windows on the front of the elementary school

MINUS

The number of parking spots in front of the print shop

... and so on. Work out about a dozen problems and then calculate the answer. Double-check your answer. The first team to return home with the right answer wins! (If the first ones back don't have the correct answer, they can head out and try again.)

CHAPTER SEVENTEEN

FAMILY MEMORIES NIGHT

"We do not remember days...we remember moments."
—Cesare Pavese

Some family evenings are for creating new memories and some are for remembering wonderful times from the past. Nothing brings a family closer than recalling and celebrating the shared experiences that are part of a family journey. Whether you decide to watch old home movies or turn vacation photos into placemats or pillowcases, take an evening to stroll, skip, or dash down memory lane with your kids.

Make a funniest-thing-that-ever-happened book

Start a family notebook for funny memories. You can spend a Family Fun Night decorating the cover with a collage of photographs and words cut out of magazines. Keep it in a central location and when something funny happens, whether it's a little sibling saying "babing suit" or someone forgetting to add sugar to the pumpkin pie at Thanksgiving, write it down. Every year on New Year's Eve, read all of the entries from the previous 12 months.

Make placemats with vacation memorabilia

Remind your kids about all of the fun they've had on family vacations by making 11" x 17" collages out of photographs, ticket stubs, brochures, restaurant napkins—anything and everything you saved from the trip. The kids can even draw pictures of things they remember. Photocopy and laminate each one at an office supply store to create lasting placemats as reminders of family fun.

Make a family time capsule

Preserve some family memories in a time capsule! You can purchase a time capsule that will last for many generations or simply put items in a plastic storage bin and tuck it up on a shelf for a designated number of years. Add things like family photos, a favorite recipe, a t-shirt from a race or event, pages from the newspaper, a wrapper from your favorite food, drawings or letters—anything that represents your family or the year that you are putting things away. It's especially meaningful for everyone to write a letter to his or her future self. As each person puts an item into the time capsule, he can explain the importance of it and why he wants to preserve it.

Record an older relative telling stories

Spend an evening with grandparents or other older relatives and record them recalling tales of their youth. Kids should arrive with questions to prompt them like, "What's the funniest thing you remember your father doing?" or "What's the most trouble you got into when you were young?" Later, you can edit the interview on the computer and post it for other family members to watch.

Write funny captions for family photos

Enlarge a particularly funny or unique photo of each member of the family and draw enough speech bubbles so that each person can write a "quote." You can put them in a scrapbook or turn them into placemats (see earlier entry).

Set aside an evening for storytelling

Storytelling is a lost art, but you can help revive it. Talk to your kids about things you remember from your own childhood, from when they were younger, or just interesting tales that you want to share. Experts advise that you tell stories you love in your own style and voice that have a clear beginning, middle, and end. Speak more slowly and louder than you think you need to, using gestures that feel natural.

MY STORY

"Just before she graduated from high school, my daughter opened a time capsule that she had put together in first grade. She had a wonderful time looking at everything she'd saved, and she actually used the letter she wrote back then as inspiration for a speech she delivered at her graduation."

—Cindy, mother of three

Share your memories with loved ones

Share photos with your extended family and far-away friends by creating an online photo album. Just email the link to your album and others can enjoy the photos from your last vacation—or your last Family Fun Night!

(Not all photo-sharing sites are free, so be sure to read the fine print—or just create an album via your social media account.)

Put your mug on a mug!

Upload your digital pictures to one of the links we recommend on www.FamilyFunNight.org to create one-of-a-kind mugs, photo books, pillowcases, cards, calendars, key chains, or even mouse pads! It's easy to do and relatively inexpensive.

Create scrapbook pages

Keep scrapbooking supplies (scissors, glue sticks, thin markers, stickers, stamps...) in a special box and let each child design his own page. Make copies of photos so that kids can cut, crop, and trim as much as they want to. Put all the pages together when you're done for a truly memorable scrapbook.

Make stepping-stones

Using a mix like Quikrete, follow the instructions to create concrete. Scoop the concrete into old pie plates, smoothing the top with a scrap of wood. Wait about an hour and a half, then let every member of the family customize one stone with beach glass, shells, pebbles, and other small weather-proof items. Cover each stone with a dishcloth and spray each with water a few times every day to cure them. In a few days, they will be ready to set outside.

INDEX

ABOUT THE AUTHOR

Cynthia L. Copeland is the *New York Times* bestselling author of more than 25 books for parents and children; she has sold over a million books in eight languages. Her work has been featured on *Good Morning America*, selected for Oprah's "O List" in O magazine, recommended by Ann Landers, and featured in the *Wall Street Journal*. She lives in New Hampshire with her family.

needs glasses but pretends she doesn't →

talks too fast because she is easily excited

lives in → sweatshirts and pajama pants

always has a messy desk →

↙ has hair that is too long for someone her age (but is trusting best friend Mary Brett to tell her kindly when it's time to get it cut)

← has 2 holes in each ear because teenage daughter talked her into it

← is afraid of new computer

Cynthia L. Copeland
(call her "Cindy")

ABOUT CIDER MILL PRESS BOOK PUBLISHERS

Good ideas ripen with time. From seed to harvest, Cider Mill Press brings fine reading, information, and entertainment together between the covers of its creatively crafted books. Our Cider Mill bears fruit twice a year, publishing a new crop of titles each spring and fall.

VISIT US ON THE WEB AT
www.cidermillpress.com

OR WRITE TO US AT
12 Spring Street
PO Box 454
Kennebunkport, Maine 04046